The
Science
of
Sciences

THE **mananam** SERIES

(Mananam–Sanskrit for "Reflection upon the Truth")

(continued on inside back page)

THE **mananam** SERIES

The
Science
of
Sciences

CHINMAYA PUBLICATIONS
CHINMAYA MISSION WEST PUBLICATIONS DIVISION

Chinmaya Publications
Chinmaya Mission West Publications Division

P.O. Box 129
Piercy, CA 95587, USA

Distribution Office
560 Bridgetowne Pike
Langhorne, PA 19053
Phone: (215) 396-0390   Fax: (215) 396-9710
Toll Free: 1-888-CMW-READ (1-888-269-7323)
Internet: www.mananam.org
                www.chinmayapublications.org

Central Chinmaya Mission Trust
Sandeepany Sadhanalaya
Saki Vihar Road
Mumbai, India 400 072

Credits:
Editorial Advisor: *Swami Tejomayananda*
Consulting Editor: *Swami Shantananda*
Series Editors: *Margaret Dukes, Rashmi Mehrotra*
Associate Editor: *Neena Dev*
Editorial Assistant: *Vinni Soni*
Cover Graphics: *Neena Dev, David Dukes*
Inside Photos: *David and Margaret Dukes*
Production Manager: *Arun Mehrotra*

Library of Congress Control Number: 2005938365
ISBN: 978-1-880687-59-8   1-880687-59-3

Contents

Part Three

THE SCIENTISTS SPEAK

Part Four

THE SAGES SPEAK

Preface

Science is defined as the investigation and observation of natural phenomena through experimentation. It is inspired by our urge to know. We want to know the "how" and "what" of things and beings. Often this search has been directed towards trying to improve the standard of living with the belief that greater comfort would make us happier. However, in the past century, men of science persevered in their search for the truth of things and in the process gained many more insights into the Laws of Nature. The study of the universe through the related sciences of physics, biology, chemistry, astronomy, and medicine inspired scientists to look deeper into the origins of matter and its properties. Later still, physicists in their research of quantum mechanics and particle physics, began to realize that they were dealing only with the appearances of things, not with the reality behind the appearances. Therefore, they concluded that there was a need to study, not only the observed phenomena, but the observer as well.

But who and what is the observer? Since ancient times, this question captivated the minds of spiritual scientists, or rishis. It is not unusual that for thousands of years, saints and sages have asked themselves: "Who am I? What is my purpose and goal in life? How can I gain lasting happiness?" The pursuit of this particular knowledge is called Self-knowledge or, as illustrated in this book, the *Science of Sciences*. Study of the Self has always, and will always exist, because it is the study of Reality, or the Supreme Intelligence, which lies behind and infuses life into everything. It is the greatest science, because knowledge of it leads the way to the ultimate fulfillment in life — total happiness and peace.

The authors in Part One describe the Science of Sciences, also called Vedanta, and modern science and show the harmony that naturally exists between them.

Part Two looks at how the findings of modern science are beginning to meet with the timeless wisdom of the ages. We see how the scientific search for Truth is leading to unification of ideas, which, in turn, is opening up a whole new dimension of experience in medicine and other scientific disciplines.

In Part Three, we gain glimpses of the great thoughts from scientists. These great thinkers discuss ethics and morality as pertaining to science. They show that the scientific quest for knowledge produced more questions than solutions, which could only be answered by the spiritual science.

This leads us to Part Four where sages and saints continue to take up the topic of values and morality. We learn that the greatest value is to gain the vision of the oneness that permeates throughout all existence.

In this book we have indicated the relationship between modern science and the Science of Sciences. We have shown that modern science can take us so far and that only the timeless Science, the science which has been there, is there, and will always be there, can help us gain lasting fulfillment and happiness in life.

The Editors

PART ONE

Modern Science: Eternal Science

*Of all sciences, the greatest science
is the knowledge of your own Self.*

S. Radhakrisnan

There are some interesting differences between the physicists and the mystics. The mystics take existence for granted and want to get from here to there; they want to see beyond the apparition. And the physicists are likely to take non-existence for granted and want to get from there to here. The Big Bang cosmologists want to get the universe out of nothing. It's like asking us to believe that nothing made everything out of nothing. But that's not what shows in our physics. If behind what we see there were only a zero, then where would gravity come from, and electricity, and inertia? I have to side with the mystics. On observational grounds I have to take existence for granted. ...

Here let me remind you that physics and philosophy are our maps. They can be judged as true or false according to whether they correspond or do not correspond to fact. But mysticism (or religion) is a journey, and about a journey one does not ask whether it is true or false, but only where it goes. Will it take me to the goal? ... This is not a journey from one place to another in an actual world: It is a journey from one point of view to another. That is why it is often referred to as an "inner journey." It is a journey from an erroneous point of view, dictated by the genes, to a point of view from which we can see through the genetic mirage. Swami Vivekananda said that science and religion would meet and shake hands. I think that time has come.

John Dobson

I

The Science of the Spirit

by Swami Chinmayananda

Our character, and ultimately our destiny are determined by what we regularly encourage and cultivate in our minds. An intelligent choice of thoughts can transform our character as well as our lives. The entire destiny of life lies in our own hands. We can rebuild our own future. Religion is the technique by which we get our minds and intellects trained to grasp and understand the larger themes of the universe and our own place in it.

Religion is not for animals; tigers and bears have no religion. Religion is the remedy for a particular unrest felt by human beings, even when he or she has all the best that life has to offer. This science of the spirit has a very practical use for us. I am not talking of the religion of bell ringing or incense burning. I am talking of an approach to life that helps us to discover a new strength to face the challenges of life and a new courage of conviction to live honestly serving others. That which provides us with such a method for masterly living is true religion.

Religion does not attempt to improve the condition of the world. It does not aim to help us gain freedom from all needs and thus grant us a higher standard of living. Instead, it teaches us a method for creating in ourselves the equipoise to stand up to life's situations, meeting efficiently the ever-changing world of challenges. True religion imparts to us the art of living.

Scientists have learned to understand increasingly more about the secrets of nature. The results of their research have given to the age more strength, daring, and vitality. Science has conquered nature, and humankind as a result of the knowledge it has accumulated, has gained mastery over the outer world. The secret of our strength is knowledge.

Yet, despite our mastery over the outer world, we still feel unhappy and unfulfilled. The great sages of the past taught that a particular kind of knowledge can transform our lives and bring to us a fullness of satisfaction that no other endeavor yields: knowledge of our inner spiritual constitution, a knowledge that gives us mastery over our lives.

The knowledge of which the sages spoke grew out of their analysis of human beings and their contacts with the outer world. They defined the instruments that contact the world, as the body, the mind, and the intellect. Then they determined how these instruments can best be readjusted so as to bring forth greater success and happiness in our lives. This analysis is the content of all sacred textbooks, whether they belong to the traditions of Christianity, Hinduism, Judaism, Islam, Buddhism, or any other major religious persuasion.

Religion begins as a scientific reevaluation of life. Just as the material scientists retire to their laboratories to do their research, the spiritual masters have retired to the cool and silent valleys of the Himalayas or to the deserts of the Middle East to do their research on the human personality. While material scientists take the outer world as their field of investigation, the subjective scientists take their own inner world of experiences as the field of their search for truth. Scientists try to understand *"What is the world?"* Spiritual masters seek to discover *"Who or what is the human being?"*

True philosophy and science are based on life's experiences. The philosophy of the Hindus has emphasized the importance of experience more than the philosophy of the West. And in Hindu philosophy, Vedanta has the unique distinction of having based itself on the entire range of human experience — namely, the three states of waking, dream, and deep sleep.

An experience can be one's own or that of another who is a reliable authority. Let us consider modem scientific research as an example. How does scientific research proceed? Science is based on innumerable hypotheses that provide possible explanations of certain natural phenomena. As new data accumulate, the laws and theories of science may need revision. Thus, science is a growing tradition, the present research being performed on the basis of the truthfulness of past conclusions.

The scriptures represent the data gathered and conclusions arrived at by generations of sages, the scientists of the spirit. Their theories and conclusions have been confirmed as true by at least a hundred mystics in every century all over the world for many thousands of years.

Religion is the technique of perfect living, of gaining better mastery over ourselves. It is the process by which we can bring forth an effective personality out of even a person shattered by disappointments.

The transformation of Arjuna, whose dialogue with Lord Krishna constitutes the eighteen chapters of the *Bhagavad Gītā*, Hinduism's best-known scripture, is an example of how spiritual wisdom can transform one's life. Krishna's eighteen discourses cured Arjuna's life-crippling despondency and transformed him into a dynamic warrior anchored in the spirit.

An individual who has mastered himself is a living institution in this world. The world exists to serve him. He alone is the inheritor of life. This self-mastery gives a person freedom from his slavery to circumstances; no more does he come under the lashes of failures or sorrows. He, in his self-mastery, rises above the body into the noble heights of power and knowledge, worthy of becoming the king-of-kings, ever enjoying a peace and tranquility deep within himself, which is impervious to even the greatest upheaval in the outer scheme of things.

Self-Development

The message of self-mastery is one and the same in all the scriptures of the world, though each scripture may teach a different technique of self-development. If these techniques were mastered, to whatever degree possible, by all the members of a generation, we could truly enjoy the godly blessing of the scientific age in which we live. Materialism is certainly acceptable and can be a blessing to us. The comforts of the scientific age, a life made easier by the use of machines, the profits gained by harnessing natural forces — all are ours by heritage. To decry them is to insult the intelligence of humanity. But when technology becomes our master and persecutes us, we must protest.

Foolish, indeed, is that scientist who creates a Frankenstein and in his intellectual vanity lets himself be haunted by the tyrant he created, refusing to destroy him. Unless the creator of Frankenstein can find a technique of developing himself to a greater strength than his creation, he has no right to protest against any member of society raising weapons to destroy this living threat.

Individually, each person has the right to rear a tiger in his house, but if it becomes wild and a threat to the community, the individual right is negated and the community justly demands the beast's destruction. Similarly, if humanity does not grow strong enough to become master of the machines it has created, this present civilization of slavery to iron wheels pounding to the rhythm of lust shall stand condemned. But should we develop a self-mastery potent enough to rule the forces of nature we have released, then certainly we shall preserve our secular endowments and come to live, served by them, as sultans of our destiny.

The technique of self-mastery, expounded in all the great textbooks of true living, advise us not to escape from life, but to maintain an intelligent way of living, according to our circumstances in life, and to use diligently and profitably all the inner and outer situations of our life. Religion is to be practiced not only in temples, prayer rooms, or hermitages. Religion, if it is to bless us with its joy, must be lived in the office, at home, and in the government chambers.

The methods of organized religions may have become enshrouded in exaggerated claims, in confusing descriptions, and in superstitious stupidities. Besides, the methods of orthodox religions may require a restatement in the context of our times, for we find ourselves thrust into a world of unprecedented competition, where we are compelled to live a life of agitation, with impoverished mental stamina and twisted intellectual faculties.

Therefore, established religions often do not directly address us; and when we hear the call of religion, our minds fail to understand. But with a little conscious living for several months, strictly following physical, mental, and intellectual disciplines, anyone can come to a better understanding of his own religion.

I am addressing the followers of all religions who, in their enthusiasm, decry their respective religions and stand self-condemned. Whoever assimilates the logic and begins his spiritual practice (*sādhanā*) shall come to recognize the sanctity of all life and the true meaning of the religion of his birth. This is the first benefit, and there are a number of them, all finding their consummation in the glorious realization of the Divine.

II

Integrating Science
and Religion
by Ken Wilber

Huston Smith — whom many consider the world's leading authority on comparative religion — has pointed out, in his wonderful book *Forgotten Truth* that virtually all of the world's great wisdom traditions subscribe to a belief in the Great Chain of Being. Smith is not alone in this conclusion. From Ananda Coomaraswamy to René Guénon, from Fritjof Schuon to Nicholas Berdyaev, from Michael Murphy to Roger Walsh, from Seyyed Nasr to Lex Hixon, the conclusion is consistent: the core of the premodern religious world view is the Great Chain of Being.

According to this nearly universal view, reality is a rich tapestry of interwoven levels, *reaching from matter to body to mind to soul to spirit.* Each senior level "envelops" or "enfolds" its junior dimensions — a series of nests within nests within nests of Being — so that every thing and event in the world is interwoven with every other, and all are ultimately enveloped and enfolded by Spirit, by God, by Goddess, by Tao, by *Brahman,* by the Absolute itself.

As Arthur Lovejoy abundantly demonstrated in his classic treatise on the Great Chain, this view of reality has in fact "been the dominant official philosophy of the larger part of civilized humankind through most of its history." The Great Chain of Being is the worldview that "the greater number of the subtler speculative minds and of the great religious teachers [both East

9

and West] have, in their various fashions, been engaged in." This stunning unanimity of deep religious belief led Alan Watts to state flatly, "We are hardly aware of the extreme peculiarity of our own position, and find it difficult to realize the plain fact that there has otherwise been a single philosophical consensus of universal extent. It has been held by [men and women] who report the same insights and teach the same essential doctrine whether living today or six thousand years ago, whether from New Mexico in the Far West or from Japan in the Far East."

The Great Chain of Being — that is perhaps a bit of a misnomer, because, as I said, the actual view is more like the Great Nest of Being, with each senior dimension enveloping or enfolding its junior dimension(s) — a situation often described as "transcend and include." Spirit transcends but includes soul, which transcends but includes mind, which transcends but includes the vital body, which transcends but includes matter. This is why the Great Nest is most accurately portrayed as a series of concentric spheres or circles, as I have indicated in Figure 1-1.

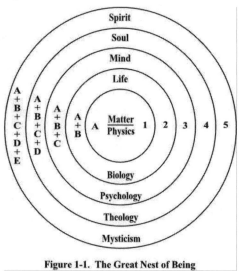

Figure 1-1. The Great Nest of Being

This is not to say that every single religious tradition from time immemorial has possessed exactly this particular scheme of matter, body, mind, soul, and spirit; there has been considerable variation within it. Some traditions have only three basic levels in the Great Nest — usually body, mind, and spirit. As Chögyam Trungpa, Rinpoche, pointed out in *Shambhala: The Sacred Path of the Warrior,* this simple hierarchy of body, mind, and spirit was nonetheless the backbone of even the earliest shamanic traditions, showing up as the hierarchy of earth, human, and heaven. This three-level scheme reappears in the Hindu and Buddhist notion of the three great states of being: *gross* (matter and body), *subtle* (mind and soul), and *causal* (spirit). Many of these traditions, on the other hand, also have extensive subdivisions of the Great Nest, sometimes breaking it down into five, seven, twelve, or even more levels and sublevels.

But the basic point has remained essentially identical: Reality is a series of nests within nests within nests, reaching from matter to mind to Spirit, with the result that all beings and all levels were ultimately enfolded in the all-pervasive and loving embrace of an ever-present Spirit.

Each senior level in the Great Nest, although it includes its juniors, nonetheless possesses emergent qualities not found on the junior level. Thus, the vital animal body *includes* matter in its makeup, but it also *adds* sensations, feelings, and emotions, which are not found in rocks. While the human mind *includes* bodily emotions in its makeup, it also *adds* higher cognitive faculties, such as reason and logic, which are not found in plants or other animals. And while the soul *includes* the mind in its makeup, it also *adds* even higher cognitions and affects, such as archetypal illumination and vision, not found in the rational mind. And so on.

In short, each higher level possesses the essential features of its lower level(s), but then adds elements not found on those levels. Each higher level, that is, *transcends* but *includes* its juniors. And this means that each level of reality has a different architecture, so to speak.

For just that reason, each level of reality, according to the great traditions, has a specific branch of knowledge associated with it (which I have also indicated in Figure 1-1): Physics studies matter. Biology studies vital bodies. Psychology and philosophy address the mind. Theology studies the soul and its relation to God. And mysticism studies the formless Godhead or pure Emptiness, the radical experience of Spirit beyond even God and the soul.

Such has been the dominant worldview, in one variation or another, for most of humankind's history and prehistory. It is the backbone of the "perennial philosophy," the nearly universal consensus about reality held by humanity for most of its time on this earth. Until, that is, the rise of modernity in the West.

The Modern Denial of Spirituality

With the rise of modernity in the West, the Great Chain of Being almost entirely disappeared. As we will see, the modern West, after the Enlightenment, became the first major civilization in the history of humanity to deny almost entirely the existence of the Great Nest of Being.

In its place was a "flatland" conception of the universe as composed basically of matter (or matter/energy), and this material universe, including material bodies and material brains, could best be studied by science, and science alone. Thus, in the place of the Great Chain reaching from matter to God, there was now matter, period. And so it came to pass that the worldview known as *scientific materialism* became, in whole or part, the dominant official philosophy of the modern West.

Many religiously minded scholars have noted this modern "collapse" of the Great Nest of Spirit, and lamented it loudly. They have blamed this collapse on everything from the Newtonian-Cartesian paradigm to patriarchal domination, from capitalistic commodification of life's values to anti-Goddess male aggression, from hatred of the holistic web of life to a devaluation of nature in favor of analytic abstractions, from material lust and greed to obsession with monetary gain. The list of malevolent causes is indeed virtually endless.

True as those explanations might be, none of them addresses the core issues. As we will *see,* there is good reason that the Great Chain in its traditional form collapsed. The Great Nest of Spirit simply could not stand up to certain undeniable truths ushered in by modernity, and if we are to integrate both premodern religion and modern science, the truths of both parties must be brought to the union. And modernity possessed a tremendous share of new truths and new discoveries — it was far from being the Great Satan.

At the same time, the rise of modernity was beset with its own grave problems, not the least of which was the massive cultural earthquake brought about by the shuddering collapse of the Great Nest of Spirit. No longer were men and women enfolded in Spirit, they were simply awash in matter: hardly a comforting universe.

So we reach a crucial point. Our aim is to integrate premodern religion with modern science. We have already seen that the core of premodern religion is the Great Nest of Being. But what exactly is the core of modernity? *If we are to integrate premodern and modern, and if premodern* is *the Great Chain, then what exactly* is *"modern"?* The key to the long-sought integration might very well lie in this neglected direction.

What Is Modernity?

What specifically did modernity bring into the world that the premodern cultures by and large lacked? What made modernity so substantially *different* from the cultures and epochs that preceded it? Whatever it was, it will have to be an essential feature of the sought-for integration.

Many answers have been offered to the question "What is modernity?" Most of them are decidedly negative. Modernity, it is said, marked the death of God, the death of the Goddess, the commodification of life, the leveling of qualitative distinctions, the brutalities of capitalism, the replacement of quality by quantity, the loss of value and meaning, the fragmentation of the lifeworld, existential dread, a rampant and vulgar materialism — all of which have often been summarized in the phrase made famous by Max Weber: "the disenchantment of the world."

No doubt there is some truth to all those claims, and we will give them abundant consideration. But clearly modernity has some immensely positive aspects as well, for it also gave us the liberal democracies; the ideals of equality, freedom, and justice, regardless of race, class, creed, or gender; modern medicine, physics, biology, and chemistry; the end of slavery; the rise of feminism; and the universal rights of humankind. Those, surely, are a little more noble than the mere "disenchantment of the world."

No, we need a specific definition or description of modernity that allows for all those factors, both good (such as liberal democracies) and bad (such as the widespread loss of meaning). Various scholars, from Max Weber to Jürgen Habermas, have suggested that what specifically defines modernity is something called "the differentiation of the cultural value spheres," which especially means the differentiation of art, morals, and science. Where previously these spheres tended to be fused, modernity differentiated them and let each proceed at its own pace, with its own dignity, using its own tools, following its own discoveries, unencumbered by intrusions from the other spheres.

This differentiation allowed each sphere to make profound discoveries that, if used wisely, could lead to such "good" results as democracy, the end of slavery, the rise of feminism, and rapid advances in medical science; but discoveries that, if used unwisely, could just as easily be perverted into the "downsides" of modernity, such as scientific imperialism, the disenchantment of the world, and totalizing schemes of world domination.

The brilliance of this definition of modernity — namely, that it differentiated the value spheres of art, morals, and science — is that it allows us to *see* the underpinnings of *both* the good news and the bad news of modernity. In ways that will become more obvious in the following chapters, [The author's book, *The Marriage of Sense and Soul*] this definition allows us to understand both the *dignity* and the *disaster* of modernity, and we will explore each of them very carefully.

Pre-modern cultures certainly possessed art, morals, and science. The point, rather, is that these spheres tended to be relatively "undifferentiated." To give only one example now, in the Middle Ages, Galileo could not freely look through his telescope and report the results because art and morals and science were all fused under the Church, and thus the morals of the Church defined what science could — or could not — do. The

Bible said (or implied) that the sun went around the earth, and that was the end of the discussion.

But with the differentiation of the value spheres, a Galileo could look through his telescope without fear of being charged with heresy and treason. Science was free to pursue its own truths unencumbered by brutal domination by the other spheres. Likewise with art and morals: Artists could, without fear of punishment, paint nonreligious themes, or even sacrilegious themes, if they wished. And moral theory was free to pursue an inquiry into the good life, whether it agreed with the Bible or not.

For all those reasons and more, these *differentiations of modernity* have also been referred to as the *dignity* of modernity, for these differentiations were in part responsible for the rise of liberal democracy, the end of slavery, the growth of feminism, and the staggering advances in the medical sciences, to name but a few of these many dignities.

As we will see, the "bad news" of modernity was that these value spheres did not just peacefully separate, they often flew apart completely. The wonderful *differentiations* of modernity went too far into actual *dissociation,* fragmentation, alienation. Dignity became disaster. The growth became a cancer. As the value spheres began to dissociate, this allowed a powerful and aggressive science to begin to invade and dominate the other spheres, crowding art and morals out of any serious consideration in approaching "reality." Science became *scientism* — scientific materialism and scientific imperialism — which soon became the dominant "official" worldview of modernity.

It was this scientific materialism that very soon pronounced the other value spheres to be worthless, "not scientific," illusory, or worse. And for precisely that reason, it was scientific materialism that *pronounced the Great Chain of Being to be nonexistent.*

According to scientific materialism, the Great Nest of matter, body, mind, soul, and spirit could be thoroughly and rudely reduced to systems of matter alone; and matter — whether in the material brain or material process systems — would account for

15

all of reality, without remainder. Gone was mind and gone was soul and gone was Spirit — gone, in fact, was the entire Great Chain, except for its pitiful bottom rung — and in its place, as Whitehead famously lamented, there was reality as "a dull affair, soundless, scentless, colorless; merely the hurrying of material, endlessly, meaninglessly."

And so it came about that the modern West was the first major civilization in the history of the human race to deny substantial reality to the Great Nest of Being. It is into this massive and universal denial that we wish to attempt to reintroduce the spiritual dimension, but on terms acceptable to science as well.

To integrate religion and science is to integrate a pre-modern worldview with a modern worldview. But we saw that the essence of pre-modernity is the Great Chain of Being, and the essence of modernity is the differentiation of the value spheres of art, morals, and science. Thus, in order to integrate religion and science, we need to *integrate the Great Chain with the differentiations of modernity.* As we will start to see in the next chapter [the author's book, *The Marriage of Sense and Soul*], this means that each of the levels in the traditional Great Chain needs to be carefully differentiated in the light of modernity. If we can do that, we will have satisfied *both* the core claim of spirituality — namely, the Great Chain — and the core claim of modernity — namely, the differentiation of the value spheres.

If this integration can be done without "cheating" — that is, without stretching and deforming either religion or science to a point where they do not recognize themselves — then this will be an integration that both parties can genuinely embrace. Such a synthesis would unite the best of pre-modern wisdom with the brightest of modern knowledge, bringing together truth and meaning in a way that has thus far eluded the modern mind.

III

Spiritual Science
by David Frawley

Spiritual science does not deny the validity or importance of outer knowledge and experimentation. It does, however, insist upon the priority of the inner knowledge over the outer. Whatever the outer knowledge provides us, it must be within the realm of time. The inner knowledge alone provides us with the means of realizing the eternal, going beyond time. As death is the most inescapable fact of our lives, it behooves us to search out the means of going beyond it. Ultimately, it does not matter if we gain all the outer goals of life like fame, wealth, talent, and genius. If we do not know ourselves we are the proverbial man who has gained the world but lost his soul. Spiritual science gives us a way to a knowledge, which allows us to know the infinite. If this is possible why should we waste away our lives on the finite?

This spiritual science is not to be confused with false imagination, superstition, with the taking of drugs or artificially induced trances. It is not a matter of wishful thinking but of the most detached inquiry. It demands the utmost seriousness, clarity and objectivity. It requires that we see through the illusions of the mind, the illusions of our self. It regards the mind itself as an illusion and our thought process as a process of illusion building unless we come to understand ourselves. It requires the highest reason and the most consummate intelligence and acuity of perception to uncover the true reality within and around us.

Nor does spiritual science exclude materialistic science.

Both have a similar rationality but applied in different directions. Spiritual science only insists that we do not apply the methods of materialistic science to the ultimate issues of life. Materialistic science works through the measurable. The ultimate issues of life — the Divine, the eternal, the infinite, bliss, and freedom — are not measurable and cannot be found by any outward examination. Spiritual science insists that we employ the appropriate instrument to know the truth of a thing. Just as a microscope will not give us a picture of the stars, so an outer oriented science, and its machines and computers, cannot show us the truth of our inner nature. We cannot find the real man by dissecting our organs or determining the electrochemical connections in the brain. This is like trying to find the light by taking apart the light bulb. The body is only our shadow. For the ultimate issues we need to know in life; who we are, what life itself is; the appropriate instrument is our own mind directed within, free from attachment or bias to any external or conditioned view. This is the great objectivity of Vedic science. ...

A Unified World-View

Spiritual science has an integral structure and a unified worldview. It is important to see how each of its aspects fit together and what the relative importance is of each. While we may use aspects of it separately, like following Ayurveda for the physical body, it is important that we do not allow our vision to be fragmented in the process.

Materialistic science is based on analysis and differentiation. Each branch of it tends to become more specialized. It requires its own language and expertise. Proficiency in one branch tends to deny proficiency in the others. For example, a biochemist cannot understand a nuclear physicist.

Spiritual science is the opposite. It is based on synthesis and integration, (*yoga*). Each branch of it tends towards the same universality. Proficiency in one aids in proficiency in the others. For example, an Ayurvedic doctor and a Vedic astrologer have a common system to communicate through. Spiritual science develops out of an integral language and approach. This is the language of the mantra, which is the language of truth perception. It is based on the root principles of the cosmic life like the five elements, the basic energetic realities of nature. Hence, to move from one branch of the spiritual sciences to another, required not the development of a new language but a shifting of the levels on which the same language and logic is applied. It is this openness of the spiritual sciences that can enable a great yogi to be a poet, philosopher, psychologist, doctor, social leader, and so on.

The Renaissance idea of the universal man is not false or impossible but requires a different way of knowledge, a different kind of thought. We must return to this synthetic knowledge if we would produce a planetary, global, or cosmic Man. The cosmic human being regards all the earth as his own, all culture and religion as belonging to himself. He has no artificial or petty barriers of country, culture, race, religion or time that bind his mind. The true knowledge unifies. The capacity of knowledge to bring us together is thereby the test of its validity. May we once more seek that and enshrine it in our hearts as well as our institutions of learning. May such seers, like the rishis of old, arise once more throughout the world!

IV

The Relevance of Religion in this Millennium

by Swami Tejomayananda

What does this millennium hold in store for us in the fields of science, education, social life, medicine, and religion? This is a question that is occupying the minds of many thinkers. The last few centuries have yielded phenomenal progress, particularly in the field of science and technology. Man has ventured far out into space trying to unravel the mysteries of the universe. Technology has made travel possible at a speed faster than sound. Computers and satellites have opened new avenues of communication. Medical research has produced amazing results. Modern warfare is more accurate and devastating than in past wars. All these advances have increased the pace of life. Man is forced to rethink various and many issues in the light of these new discoveries. Questions regarding euthanasia, cloning, morality and ethics demand immediate answers. These changes are affecting political, social, and economic equations.

While it appears that there has been marvelous progress in various avenues, paradoxically we see increased destruction and violence in many places. The old value systems are degenerating. Families are breaking down, leading to a lot of mental distress. People are more unruly and violent. Nations are itching for conflict at the first opportunity. At this rate, what will happen in this millennium? In particular, what will happen with religion? Change is the changeless law of the world. With each change in the past — for example, the Industrial Revolution, the First World War, the Second World War — came a dwarfing of the previous change, each always being a great phenomenon, influencing the lives of millions. And, yet, the fundamental principles of living remained unchanged. Religion has played its role in the past. The question is: Will religion be of any consequence in this new millennium? What will be its position? Will it have any relevance in the future way of life? If it has relevance, what form will it take?

The relevance of any thing is determined by the need and purpose it serves. For example, even though change takes place in the outside world, our hunger and thirst remains. Hence, there will always be the need for food. To produce food we will require farming. Though the methods of farming will change, the science of agriculture will remain relevant, because it fulfills a need. Different branches of medicine may appear and disappear, but the science of medicine will remain relevant as long as the body is afflicted with disease. Similarly, people require governance. Hence, politics with all its branches of administration will remain relevant. Man is not just a physical being. He has thoughts, emotions, and a keen aesthetic sense. Hence, philosophy, along with science, art, music, and dance, will be relevant. When one thinks along these lines one will understand that religion will also remain relevant. The question is: What is religion? What role does it play in one's life?

Aspects of Religion

Religion has the following three aspects:
1. Philosophy: Philosophy refers to the vision of Truth. It is the vision of the entirety of life. This aspect will be relevant for all those who are the seekers of Truth. Their desires go beyond interests in food, clothing and shelter, vain entertainment, or sensual pleasures. From time immemorial, many

seekers of Truth renounced all material objects and went in the search for Truth. Such people came from different backgrounds of society, and with an intense longing to know the Truth. At the highest level, religion fulfills this demand. The purpose of religion is to enlighten people about their own nature and the nature of the Absolute Truth of life. As long as there are seekers of Truth, there will be a religion that fulfills this demand, and that religion will always remain relevant.

2. Moral and Ethical Values: Values are a very important aspect of religion, as moral and ethical values keep a society integrated and in harmony. Society consists of individuals, and the health of a society depends upon the quality of education of each person. Education not only involves gaining knowledge and the skill to apply this knowledge in life but it also includes understanding the purpose of this knowledge. For example, after the completion of the medical course, doctors take an oath that they will use this knowledge to serve society. So, the knowledge that one gathers should be used to enrich and serve society. Earlier the focus of business was only on how to make a profit, but now they have realized that one cannot make a profit without taking care of the customer's interest. In the beginning, management used force and authority, but now it is slowly changing to management by love. This also is an aspect of religion. For all moral and ethical values, the basis is the vision of the Oneness of the Self, which is gained through religion. However materialistic a society may become, even such a society will have to abide by the principle of "live and let live." As one ponders one's own happiness, one will also have to look upon the other person's happiness. When one deceives someone else, one is deceiving one's own self. Therefore, one should have moral values, otherwise one's own existence will be in danger. These values will always remain relevant. Without this aspect of religion there cannot be any peace, harmony and integration in society.

3. Rituals, Customs, and Traditions: Rituals are a demonstration of the philosophical vision. Customs and traditions are also derived from the same vision. This aspect of religion has great potential for changes and variations. Everyone cannot understand the vision theoretically. Some require demonstrations. And so, many rituals came into existence to demonstrate the vision. When people follow them, they learn the significance of what they are doing, which enables them to slowly turn their minds towards the Highest Truth. This aspect of religion differs greatly from one religion to another, to the extent that it gives a feeling that religions are totally different from one another. Even in a single religion, numerous denominations exist, often competing with one another. Then comes the sense of superiority and inferiority. The wars that are fought in the name of religion are not prompted by religion, but more by a belief that one's religion is superior and an insistence that others should join that religion.

Looking back at the history of religion, specifically Hinduism, one does not know when it began or who the founder was. All other religions were established in a particular historical period with a specific founder. Over the course of time, each religion changed vastly, branching into various sects and denominations, each with its own founder. This is inevitable because people change and their appreciation of things also changes. Industrialization, too, has brought many changes in society. While the form and nature of religion have to change; the vision of Truth and the values based on it will remain permanent. The religion that understands the ever-changing nature of this world and is able to modify itself at the empirical level — keeping the basic nature intact — will survive. Those that become rigid and are unable to change will perish.

One thing is certain, religion existed in the past, it exists now, and it will always exist. Certain countries or governments have tried to do away with religions by closing down temples and other places of worship, but had to reopen them. The spirit cannot be killed. At times, the voice of the spirit may seem feeble, and the number of seekers may decrease, but their power will remain unshaken. Religion can never become irrelevant. We do not know the form it will take in this millennium. We may see some kind of synthesis of the various aspects of different religions, perhaps giving birth to a new religion for all. Masters have tried to bring synthesis among religions, but they succeeded only in adding a new religion. If one thinks that by taking something from Hinduism, Islam, Christianity, Buddhism, and so forth, one can have a new Universal Religion, it is unlikely to happen. In a way, every religion has taken some aspects of other religions, but still they continue to maintain their individuality. This is a strange phenomenon.

Above all, we should understand the true essence of religion as the oneness of the Self. All moral and ethical values should be based on this understanding. Furthermore, if we base our lives on these values, then the world would become a better place. Many wrong notions and confusions may arise, and some may try to destroy the very foundation of religion. But those who understand the Truth must abide in it and become strong in it.

V

The Harmony between Science and Religion

by Thomas J. McFarlane

About the same time the Buddha lived in India, the first Western philosophers planted the seeds of science in ancient Greece. Chief among them, Pythagoras proposed that the entire cosmos was mathematically ordered and could be rationally understood in terms of numbers and their relationships. Although this seed took centuries to sprout, it was — and still is — at the root of the scientific approach to understanding reality. Nearly 2000 years later, during the Renaissance, Pythagoras' notion was linked to the experimental method, and science as we know it was born.

Most historians would agree that animosity between science and religion in Western culture first arose when scientific thinkers like Copernicus and Galileo made discoveries that seemed to flatly contradict the religious dogma of the day. As a consequence, those who would further scientific knowledge were condemned as heretics by the church. Later, as the power of science increased, reality was divided into material and spiritual halves, and science was given authority over the material world. This artificial division between religion and science, in turn, gave rise to several misconceptions that are commonly held to this day.

One such misconception is that science deals with physical facts, while religion deals with spiritual values. Science, we are told, tells us what facts are true, while religion tells us what values are good. Yet when science makes a statement of fact, it is also making a judgment about what is valuable. If a golden nugget is found to be fool's gold, all its value suddenly vanishes; in the same way, if science declares the material world to be the only reality, it implicitly challenges the value of any spiritual reality. What we take to be scientific fact determines what we value. Also, what we value helps determine what we consider to be scientific facts. We see this especially when two very different theories explain the same experimental data. In that case, scientists choose one theory over the other by appeal to values such as beauty, elegance, simplicity, and coherence.

Facts, as well as values, are also essential to religion. The essential core of any system of spiritual values is the true nature of reality. For mystics, Buddha nature, *Brahman* or the Tao are not just the ultimate value but the ultimate fact, reality and truth. Knowledge of this truth is the key to salvation or liberation. As Jesus said, "Ye shall know the truth, and the truth shall make you free." Or, as the Buddha put it, "One who acts on truth is happy in this world and beyond." Both facts and values are inseparable elements of religion as well as science.

Another misconception is that science deals with the outer, material world, while religion deals with the inner, spiritual world. Actually, scientific theories are shaped not only by our perceptions of the outer world but also by the scientist's aesthetic sensibilities such as mathematical beauty, elegance, simplicity and coherence. The ultimate object of scientific knowledge is not the external world seen through the senses but a theory of the world's order and harmony as perceived in the scientist's mind.

Although the mind is the primary tool used in religious contemplation, the scope of such contemplation includes both inner and outer objects. The ultimate goal of the spiritual seeker is to recognize that there is no real distinction between inner and outer, self and other. Religious traditions, as well as scientific thought, deal with both the internal world of insights and the external world of sensory phenomena.

Nor is it accurate to say that science is based on rational thought and doubt, while religion is based on intuition and faith.

It is true that reason and logic are important standards of scientific thought; yet not a single great creative scientific breakthrough would have been possible without intuitive insight and inspiration. And while intuitive insight is the fountain of all sacred teachings, rational thought and philosophical reasoning play important roles in clearing the mind so intuition can shine without obstruction.

Similarly, although the scientist must be willing to doubt every physical hypothesis, the practice of science calls for fundamental faith that reality is rationally comprehensible. The spiritual seeker, too, must begin with faith that the ultimate truth can be known, but will never know that truth without a radical doubt of all human forms of knowledge. Both faith and doubt, as well as logic and intuition, are qualities that the scientist and the mystic share in common.

Dissolving Artificial Distinctions

Artificial distinctions between science and religion, once dissolved, reveal the harmony between them. The Good and True are united, Plato tells us. The Upanishads declare that the inner *Atman* and the outer *Brahman* are identical. There is a deep level of reality that both outer and inner, fact and value, share in common. Knowing this reality requires reason and intuition, doubt and faith. As two complementary approaches to the same reality, science and religion can combine their observational techniques with concepts and symbols that may give rise to revolutionary new cosmologies and theories.

Both scientists and mystics investigate reality by refining their capacities to observe extremely subtle phenomena far beyond the limits of ordinary perception. Physics constructs elaborate measuring devices and uses mathematical symbols to represent reality. The contemplative traditions cultivate special forms of insight through meditation and other mental disciplines and use myth, art, poetry, parable and philosophy to represent reality.

THOMAS J. MCFARLANE

One difference is that mystics view their doctrines as ultimately pointing to a reality that cannot be known in concept or theory, while scientists are concerned with developing conceptual models of an objective reality. Their goal is not reality itself but a theory about reality. This difference, however, is not essential to an opposition between science and religion. Most spiritual teachings and experiences are not about the ineffable Absolute but relate to what can be objectively known. The same is true of science.

By comparing the scientific and contemplative approaches to reality, we can see the possibilities for convergence. Einstein and Buddha both sought to know the deepest truths about the same reality, using many of the same investigative principles. It's no wonder they had similar things to say about what they discovered.

VI

The Science of
Human Beings in Depth
by Swami Ranganathananda

Several biologists tell us today that we do not know much about the science of the human being in depth. We are only scratching the surface of this great science. Whereas this is the science that India developed ages ago in its *adhyātma-vidyā*—the science of spirituality. It proclaimed that behind this body-mind complex there is a vast, infinite reservoir of energy, which we can unfold and manifest. That is the meaning of the science of religion. Religion can be treated as an ethnic or a tribal phenomenon. That is how we deal with religion today — Hindu, Muslim, Christian, and so forth. These are ethnic and socio-political expressions of religion, but religion has another aspect — it is a science, a science of man in depth, dealing with man's spiritual growth and all the blessings that follow from that growth. This can be studied, controlled, communicated, checked, and verified.

The Upanishads developed this profound science of man in depth, so that a human being can grow beyond the limitations placed by the organic system. The individual can overcome these limitations. He or she can become a locus of freedom within this universe. Nothing in the world is free; even in man, the body is not free. There is some focus of freedom beyond the body-mind complex, beyond the cause and effect determinism. That wonderful focus must be realized. India called it the focus of God, the *Ātman*. The word "God," which appeared in religion before, had its own meanings. But, here, a new special meaning is given to whatever you call God — the eternal, immortal, infinite Consciousness, one and non-dual. Where do you seek it? Seek it in the individual, seek for it in the core of his or her being; not only because it is there, but the human being has the organic capacity to pursue this search, just like it has the organic capacity to pursue the search for the nuclear dimension of matter in the external world.

God, so understood, is called *Brahman* or *Ātman* by the Upanishads. It is of the nature of infinite Consciousness, or *cit svarūpa*, one and non-dual. It projects the universe and all living beings, maintains it, and, at the end of a cosmic cycle, withdraws all to Itself, till a new cycle of creation begins. The main thrust of this teaching is that *Brahman* or *Ātman* is present in the universe and the evolution of the universe, first cosmic, then organic, and finally spiritual, is a gradual manifestation of the *Ātman* or *Brahman. The uniqueness of the human species is that it has developed the capacity to realize* Brahman *or* Ātman*, the very source of the whole universe.* This supreme human uniqueness, which no other evolutionary species has, is described by *Śrīmad Bhāgavatam* in a significant phrase: "endowed with the intelligence to realize *Brahman.*"[1]

No animal created science, only the human being has created science. Because he or she has the capacity to train the mind, to understand the truth that is there. But truth is not open; you have to break open the outer crust of nature and discover what is there. You have to knock at the door of nature. This training of the human mind in search of truth is a common training for physical science and the science of spirituality. You have only to change the plane of search. So, in ancient India, after some advancement in physical sciences like mathematics, astronomy, metallurgy, medicine, surgery, linguistics, and so forth, and concepts of the immensity of time and space, highly trained minds invested their energies in this new field of investigation, namely, the inner nature of the human being. They found no conflict between this as well as that. It is only a continuous process and external or internal are merely names without any significance so far as the truth is concerned. We make an artificial distinction between nature external and nature internal only for the purposes of study and research. We take this body as a measuring rod and say: "This truth is outside, and this is inside." Truth is like space; it has no internal or external; but we do make that distinction for practical purposes only. Space is indivisible; so is truth.

So, our ancient teachers said that there is some reality, some truth, hidden somewhere. We make it external or internal for the purpose of study, but after the study is over, we should not continue in that distinction; so, break down these barriers. Just like the ocean surrounding the earth — we call it Atlantic, Pacific, and so forth; but the earth knows only one ocean. In that way, our teachers said, let us pursue truth first in the external world. That is the most obvious aspect of reality that confronts us at the very time of our birth. We should continue the search and go deep into the human being, into the depth of consciousness, into the subject of the self, what is behind this self, what is the nature of this consciousness? Is man merely this tiny organic system? Or, is there something profound within himself — man the unknown? The American scientist Alexis Carell, early in this century, wrote a book, *Man the Unknown.* That is a remarkable field of search.

Unification of Science

In the Upanishads, therefore, this great science of the human being in depth was developed. As a result, India treated it as a continuation of the search for truth outside by her physical sciences. No two sciences can conflict with each other. This unification of knowledge external and knowledge internal is what is unique about Vedanta. Lord Krishna refers to it in the *Bhagavad Gītā*[2]:

> This body is called *kṣetra* or field, O son of Kunti; the one who knows this body (and its source in external nature) is called the *kṣetrajña* or the knower of the *kṣetra* by those who know it.

> Know Me (the Divine Incarnation) to be the *kṣetrajña* or "Knower of the *Kṣetra*" in all the *kṣetra*, O Bharata. The (unified) knowledge of *kṣetra* and *kṣetrajña is* (true) knowledge, according to My view.

The knowledge of the *kṣetra* and the *kṣetrajña* — the unified knowledge of both is called *jñāna*, or knowledge in the true sense of the term, says Lord Krishna. The body and its source, representing the external world (the not-self) and the Knower of the body representing the internal world (the Self) — both we have to know. That alone is full knowledge. Thus alone can you comprehend the totality of Reality, Reality in its wholeness. The Upanishads in one place spoke of truth and the Truth of truth — *satyam* and *satyasya satyam*. That is how Vedanta developed its approach to truth. One of the statements given in the *Muṇḍaka Upaniṣad* is that Vedanta is *sarva-vidyā-pratiṣṭhā,* a science that is the basis of every *vidyā* or science. There is a unity behind this diversity. That unity must be discovered. That can be discovered first by studying nature outside. Whatever conclusions you come to by that outside investigation is perfectly fine; but it will be inconclusive. Then you study the inside of nature as revealed in the human being. This is also a real scientific investigation. Vedanta discovered that unity. In the Introduction to his commentary on the *Brahma Sūtra,* Shankara refers to this discovery thus: "All Upanishads commence with the search for the science of the unity of the Self."

It is not a creed or a dogma meant for believing. You can test it for yourself. What is the true dimension of the human being? Is it merely this physical system, or this nervous system, or the psychic system? Go deep; try to pierce into these aspects. In fact, today's biology has already isolated three types of sheaths or coverings in nature. One is the ordinary nature, which you see outside, for which we use the word physical sphere; the second is the hydrosphere; and the third, atmosphere. That is understood in biology, physics and chemistry. Then there is a biosphere, the world can be seen through that angle; then there is a psychic sphere.

The Five Sheaths

In sociology, you have to deal with this psychic sphere. When I deal with you, I am dealing with a common medium by which I communicate. This is called a mind-field, as we say in physics. In sociology, without that mind-field, we cannot handle inter-relationships between human beings. It is not that just two individual physical systems are reacting; there is some thing subtler than that, and beyond the physical system, and is able to intertwine with other systems that are there. This study in sociology reveals a deep dimension of the human being. Says the American biologist George Gaylord Simpson, in his *The Meaning of Evolution*:

> A broad classification of the sciences into physical, biological, and social corresponds with three levels of organization of matter and energy, and not levels only, but also quite distinct kinds of organization. The three are of sharply increasing orders of complexity and each includes the lower grades. Vital organization is more intricate than physical organization, and it is added to and does not replace physical organization, which is also fully involved in vital organization. Social organization retains and sums up the complexities of both these and adds its own still greater complexities.[3]

The Upanishads discovered the five sheaths covering the infinite *Ātman*. The Upanishadic sages, therefore, said: Study this human system in depth. One whole *Upaniṣad*, the *Taittirīya*, is devoted to this study — that a human being consists of five sheaths or *kośa: annamaya, prāṇamaya, manomaya, vijñānamaya,* and *ānandamaya* going inwards, the innermost is the ultimate Reality, *Brahman* or *Ātman*, of the nature of infinite Consciousness, One and non-dual. It is like a sword in a sheath. The sheath is not the sword; it looks like a sword. Then add four more sheaths, which are more and more subtle; ultimately, there is the sword. That sword is the example for the true Self.

Just as Simpson said in the passage quoted above, the Upanishad even mentions that each succeeding sheath includes the previous sheath and does not replace it: the succeeding one fills the preceding one.

In this way, a tremendous investigation was undertaken into the nature of the human being by the Vedantic sages, by piercing through these external coverings, and they discovered a profound truth that the imperishable Reality that is called God by religions is hidden in every human being. The human being is essentially divine. This is a great truth, discovered and re-authenticated, and meant to be realized by every human being. It is not merely to be believed in, that comes again and again in the Vedantic literature. Not only are we divine, but we can also realize this Truth. And that realization will give us a fulfillment, which nothing else can give. I may own the whole world. I may acquire knowledge from here and there, but unless this realization comes, the sense of fulfillment will not come to me. So, this is how they investigated this subject, and, as I said, there is a smooth transition from the external to the internal, as the external search did not give conclusive answers. About the inconclusiveness of the conclusion of all physical sciences, Sir James Jeans says:

> Physical science sets out to study a world of matter and radiation and finds that it cannot describe or picture the nature of either, even to itself. Protons, electrons, and neutrons have become as meaningless to the physicists as X, Y, are to a child on its first day of learning algebra. The most we hope for at the moment is to discover ways of manipulating X, Y, Z without knowing what they are, with the result that the advance of knowledge is at present reduced to what Einstein has described as extracting one incomprehensible from another incomprehensible.[4]

This is what Vedanta calls *māyā*. It does not mean that the world does not exist. It is what Shankara says in his *Vivekacūḍāmaṇi* (verse 109): "A great wonder or mystery, and of the nature of uncertainty or indeterminacy."

FOOTNOTES:

1 *Śrīmad Bhāgavatam*, 11.9.28.
2 *Bhagavad Gītā*, 13:1-2.
3 George Gaylord Simpson, *The Meaning of Evolution*, p. 312.
4 *The New Background of Science*, p. 68.

PART TWO

Modern Science : Eternal Science
Coming Closer

*The sole concern of learning is
to seek one's original heart.*

Mencius

Facts are a historian's stock in trade, and he has to acquire them in quantities that would be repellant if the facts did not fascinate him. I love the facts of history, but not for their own sake. I love them as clues to something beyond them — as clues to the nature and meaning of the mysterious universe in which every human being awakes to consciousness. We wish to understand the universe and our place in it.

We know that our understanding of it will never be more than a glimmer, but this does not discourage us from seeking as much light as we can win. Curiosity may be focused on anything in the universe; but the spiritual reality behind the phenomena is, I believe, the ultimate objective of all curiosity; and it is in virtue of this that curiosity has something divine in it.

Arnold Toynbee
in The Saturday Review April 5, 1959

VII

Māyā and Space-Time
by Swami Jitatmananda

One of the fundamental concepts of *Advaita Vedānta* is its theory of *Maya*. It is also its most controversial one. *Maya* is not mere illusion or ignorance understood in a worldly sense. Swami Vivekananda correctly characterized it as "a statement of fact." "What you call matter or spirit or mind or anything else you may like to call them, the fact remains the same, we cannot say that they are, we cannot say they are not ... a fact, yet at the same time, not a fact. This is a statement of facts, and this is what is called *Maya*."[1]

Shankara had identified *Maya* with space, time and causation — *deśa, kāla, nimitta*. Swami Vivekananda followed Shankara's theory of *Maya* but gave it a thoroughly modern logical formulation. Long before Einstein, he clearly stated the relativity of time and space. In the following statement he advances concepts that come so very close to those of Einstein:

> The one peculiar attribute we find in time, space and causation is that they cannot exist separate from things. Try to think of space without color or limits or any connection with the things around — just abstract space. You cannot. You have to think of it as the space between two limits, or between three objects. It has to be connected with some object to have any existence. So with time; you cannot have any idea of abstract time [or absolute time, as Einstein put it — *author*] but you have to take two events by the idea of succession. Time depends on two events, just as space has to be related to outside objects. And the idea of causation is inseparable from time and space.[2]

Maya was posited by Shankara in order to explain the existence of the phenomenal universe. The theory of *Maya* was a logical necessity. At the same time, he could not deny the principle of evolution in the phenomenal world. To reconcile evolution with *Maya*, the followers of Shankara developed the doctrine of Apparent Transformation (*vivarta vāda*). Dualists like the followers of *Sāṁkhya* and theists, adopted the doctrine of Real Transformation (*pariṇāma vāda*) according to which the world is the result of actual transformation of the ultimate reality. Explaining the *vivarta vāda* Swami Vivekananda stated:

> According to the Advaitist proper, the followers of Shankaracharya, the whole universe is the apparent evolution of God. God is the material cause of this universe, but not really, only apparently. The celebrated illustration used is that of the rope and the snake, where the rope appeared to be the snake, but was not really so. The rope did not really change into the snake. Even so, this whole universe as it exists is that Being. It is unchanged, and all the changes we see in it are only apparent. These changes are caused by space, time and causation (*deśa, kāla,* and *nimitta*) or, according to a higher psychological generalization, by name and form (*nāma* and *rūpa).* It is only by name and form that one thing is differentiated from another. Again, it is not, the Vedantists say, that there is something as phenomenon and something as noumenon. The rope is changed into the snake apparently only; and when the delusion ceases, the snake vanishes.[3]

Māyā *and Consciousness*

It is doubtful whether Einstein would have gone so far with Vivekananda in accepting the theory of *Maya*. But another great physicist, Erwin Schrödinger, did. In a famous talk he gave at the Cambridge University soon after the Second World War, Schrödinger said:

> Consciousness is never experienced in the plural, only in the singular... How does the idea of plurality (so emphatically opposed by the Upanishad writers) arise at all?

Consciousness finds itself intimately connected with, and dependent on, the physical state of a limited region of matter, the body... Now there is a great plurality of similar bodies. Hence the pluralization of consciousness or minds seems a very suggestive hypothesis. Probably all simple, ingenuous people, as well as the great majority of Western philosophers, have accepted it. The only possible alternative is simply to keep the immediate experience that consciousness is a singular of which the plural is unknown, that there is only one thing and that, what seems to be a plurality, is merely a series of different aspects of this one thing produced by a deception (the Indian *Maya*) — the same illusion is produced in a gallery of mirrors, and in the same way Gaurishankar and Mt. Everest turned out to be the same peak seen from different valleys.[4]

We have seen that Einstein's greatest achievement consisted not in showing that everything is relative but in discovering the way to truth through the relative world, in establishing the absolute validity of fundamental physics laws in spite of relativity. In a similar way, Vedanta does not simply describe the world as *Maya* and leaves you there, but shows you the way to the Truth, the absolute nature of Consciousness.

Einstein abandoned the hypothesis of ether in his search for higher truth, higher generalization. The Indian sages too had discovered something similar to ether, the elemental *ākāśa*, but they went far beyond that and discovered Consciousness as the ultimate Reality: *prajñānāma brahma*. Says Swami Vivekananda:

If the theory of ether failed in ancient times to give a solution of the mystery of the universe, working out the details of that ether theory would not bring us much nearer to the truth... What I mean is that, in inquiry into the principle, the Hindu thinkers were as bold as, and in some cases much bolder than, the moderns. They made some of the grandest generalizations that have yet been reached, and some still remain as theories, which modern science has yet to get even as theories. For instance, they not only arrived at the ether theory, but went beyond and classified mind also as a still more rarefied ether. Beyond that again, they found a still more rarefied ether. Yet that was no solution, it did not solve the problem.[5]

They found the solution by going beyond even the more rarefied ether or *Maya*, and by discovering the Absolute — the infinite, immutable, non-dual consciousness beyond all relativity, beyond all contradiction. Wherever there is contradiction there is relativity, there is *Maya*. The great first-century Buddhist philosopher Nagarjuna used the attribute of contradictoriness to show the illusory nature of the phenomenal world. Teachers of *Advaita Vedānta* went one step further and using non-contradictoriness as the test of absolute truth, discovered *Brahman* as the ultimate Reality.

The Contradictory Nature of the World

Modern physics has ended in the finding that the apparently hard reality of matter is, in the quantum world, a mere shadow. Electron is only a "probability wave." And this concept leads, says physicist Fritjof Capra, "to another pair of opposite concepts which is even more fundamental, that of existence and non-existence...we can never say that an atomic particle exists at a certain place, nor can we say it does not exist. Being a probability pattern, the particle has tendencies to exist in various places and thus manifests a strange kind of physical reality between existence and nonexistence."[6]

These words seem like an echo of what Vivekananda said in London at the end of the last century, "This world has no existence." What is meant by that? It means that it has no absolute existence. It exists only in relation to my mind, your mind and to the mind of everyone else."[7]

Nobel physicist Robert Oppenheimer expresses this basic contradiction, this fundamental incertitude in our knowledge of the world: "If we ask, for instance, whether the position of the electron remains the same, we must say 'no'; if we ask whether the electron is at rest we must say 'no'; if we ask whether it is in motion, we must say 'no'."[8]

These words seem like an echo of what an ancient Upanishadic seer uttered with equal force about *Brahman*, the ultimate Reality behind the phenomenal world:

It moves. It moves not.
It is far, and yet it is near
It is within all this
And it is outside all this.[9]

The *Katha Upaniṣad* describes the ultimate Reality as "smaller than the smallest and yet greater than the greatest." In the same strain writes the Christian Mystic Nicholas de Cusa: "...the walls of the Paradise in which Thou Lord dwellest is built of contradictories." And Dionysius the Areopagite: "He is both at the root and in motion, and yet is in neither state."[10] "Thus we find," says Vivekananda, "that *Maya* is not a theory for the explanation of the world. It is simply a statement of facts as they exist, that the very basis of our being is contradiction, that everywhere we have to move through this tremendous contradiction."[11]

A man walking on the desert continues to see a lake although he knows it is only a mirage. The physicist tries to look at a subatomic object as particles although he realizes that the particle has already dematerialized into what particle physicists describe as "interconnected patterns of dynamic energy", or, as physicist David Bohm likes to call it, a "holon," a particle holographically connected with the entire universe. The whole universe is an "implicate order," as Bohm puts it, where there is always a deeper unity underlying the surface. The individual electron as a particle is thus both real and unreal. The microcosm may sometimes behave as a particle, and sometimes it may also indicate that it is an inextricable part of the macrocosm. Modern physics has stepped into the world of a number of bewildering contradictions where particles behave as waves, and waves as particles; where a single particle is also a reflection of the whole universe; where objective reality, though apparently real is yet illusory; where we know what happens at the end of the reaction, but never know in exactitude how it happens, because subatomic phenomena are like "an unopenable watch," as Einstein said. To be aware of these basic contradictions in our knowledge of Reality, and in life, is to be aware of *Maya*. The struggle to go beyond the contradictions is the spiritual struggle. To succeed in this struggle is the attainment of liberation (*Nirvāṇa* or *Samādhi*). But as long as we act, live, and think in this eversense-bound world, we shall be compelled to live only in the midst of everlasting contradictions, which go by the name *Maya*.

Vivekananda exposes the inescapable limitations of our intellect and the indomitable desire for knowledge in men struggling in a world of space-time-causality.

> So with our intellect. In our desire to solve the mysteries of the universe, we cannot stop our questioning, we feel we must know and cannot believe that no knowledge is to be gained. A few steps, and there arises the wall of beginningless and endless time which we cannot surmount. A few steps, and there appears a wall of boundless space which cannot be surmounted, and the whole is irrevocably bound by the walls of cause and effect. We cannot go beyond them. Yet we struggle, and still have to struggle. And this is *Maya*.[12]

How to go beyond *Maya*? How to resolve contradictions? Vedanta says — by realizing that Absolute is above and beyond the contradictions of the world of *Maya*. And this Absolute is not a personal God sitting somewhere on the clouds, but the self-luminous infinite consciousness everpresent inside every being. It is only by realizing the Absolute within that all contradiction ceases. This is the unanimous declaration of all the Upanishads. And Vivekananda concludes his exposition of *Maya* with this very idea of the Absolute within each of us.

> We see, then, that beyond this *Maya* the Vedantic philosophers find something that is not bound by *Maya*; and if we can get there, we shall not be bound by *Maya*. This idea is in some form or other the common property of all religions. But, with Vedanta, it is only the beginning of religion and not the end. The idea of Personal God, the Ruler of *Maya*, or nature, is not the end of these Vedantic ideas; it is only beginning. The idea grows and grows until the Vedantist finds that he who, he thought, was standing outside, is he himself and is in reality within.[13]

Attempts to go beyond the phenomenal world to the Absolute is not just a philosophical speculation. It is a part of man's spiritual quest through all the ages. Man can and does reach that stage. Says Vivekananda, "The wise person (*jñānī*) takes nothing for granted; he analyses by pure reason and force of will until he reaches Self-realization (*nirvāṇa*) which is the extinction of all relativity. No description or even conception of this state is possible." Nearly 60 years after Vivekananda's passing away, physicist David Bohm concludes his book *Causality and Chance in Modern Physics* (introduction by Nobel physicist de Broglie) with an identical observation:

> The essential character of scientific research is, then, that it moves towards the Absolute by studying the relative, in its inexhaustible multiplicity and diversity.[14]

In a sense, through Relativity and Quantum Mechanics, modern science has already reached the door of the "transcendental" realm. Writes Milic Capek: "To deny the transcendent qualities would be as uncritical as for a blind person to deny colors, for a deaf person to deny sounds, or for human beings to deny qualities which some animals undoubtedly experience under the impacts of ultrasonic waves or ultraviolet rays."[15]

FOOTNOTES:

[1] *The Complete Works of Swami Vivekananda* (Calcutta: Advaita Ashrama, 1976) Vol. 2, p. 112.

[2] *Complete Works*, Vol. 2, pp. 135-36.

[3] *Complete Works*, (1977) Vol. 1, p. 363.

[4] Erwin Schrödinger, *What is Life* (London Cambridge University Press, 1948).

[5] *Complete Works*, Vol. 2, p. 90.

[6] Fritjof Capra, *The Tao of Physics* (Berkeley: Shambhala 1973) p. 153.

[7] *Complete Works*, Vol. 2, p. 91.

[8] Quoted in *The Tao of Physics*, p. 154.

[9] *Iśa Upaniṣad*, 5.

[10] Quoted in Huston Smith, *Forgotten Truth: The Primordial Tradition* (Harper Colophone books, 1978) pp. 108-9.

[11] *Complete Works*, Vol. 2, p. 87.

[12] *Complete Works*, Vol. 2, p. 119.

[13] *Complete Works*, Vol. 2, p. 104.

[14] David Bohm, *Causality and Chance in Modern Physics* (London: Routeledge and Kegan Paul Ltd. 1957) p. 170.

[15] Milic Capek, *The Philosophical Impact of Contemporary Physics* (Princeton, New Jersey: D. Van Nostrand Co., Inc. 1961) p. 369.

VIII

Quantum Theory and Consciousness

by *Haridas Chaudhuri*

In many areas today, in many branches of science, momentous discoveries are being made. But not all of those aware of the discoveries in modern science are aware of their revolutionary philosophical impact, or revolutionary spiritual significance — of what they imply in terms of our world picture, our over-all philosophical outlook. So, I shall try to bring out for you one aspect, one important area, where we find that science and spirituality have come together joining hands in affirming an indivisible truth.

One basic problem, which we have all felt, which human beings have felt over for the last few centuries, is the disparity between the scientific view of man and the spiritual view of man. From the spiritual standpoint, man has freedom. Man is essentially a spiritual being and he has freedom. Furthermore, this freedom that man has is not an impotent kind of freedom. It is creative freedom, freedom to create new values out of the abysmal depths of his own being. That is the kind of freedom which man possesses. And this is the basic affirmation of philosophy, of religion, of mysticism.

Whereas when we turn to science, we get a different picture, not only different but a diametrically opposed picture. How? Because a scientist will tell you that man, like every other thing in this world, is subject to the universal law of cause and effect, which reigns supreme in the whole universe. Which therefore means that like everything else man also is completely determined by natural forces operating according to natural laws. And these natural forces are supposed to be blind, mechanical, and thus the scientific view emerging from the law of cause and effect is that man is a creature of circumstances and forces over which he has no control.

I want you first of all to see this dichotomy here, this duality, these two radically opposite, sharply conflicting views of man. Religion, mysticism, spirituality affirm that man as a spiritual being is free, that he has freedom. So much so that he has freedom to commit sins and make mistakes. He has that much freedom. He violates laws. He has that much freedom. On the other hand, there is the scientific view according to which man is a helpless creature of circumstances beyond his control. In other words, the mechanistic view of man and the spiritualistic view of man as a free being — this is the opposition.

However, in modern science some revolutionary discoveries are being made. One such discovery is quantum mechanics. This scientific discovery now tells us that even from the standpoint of science, man has freedom. That is a discovery of epoch-making significance, revolutionary philosophical and spiritual impact, completely shaking to the foundations old-fashioned scientific knowledge. In past times, science was regulated by the atomistic viewpoint, mechanistic outlook, reductionistic attitude — that all the higher things of life such as moral, religious, mystical spiritual phenomena can be reduced to blind forces, interaction of blind, unconscious elements of matter — atoms and molecules. That was the old-fashioned scientific outlook, summed up in this atomistic, mechanistic approach.

However, if you study and understand the discoveries of modern science, you will find that profound revolution has taken place in this outlook. The atomistic, mechanistic approach has been replaced by what is called the systems view of the universe, the organismic view of the world. This is a complete reversal of outlook, a Copernican revolution of our time. This has many implications. I shall focus my attention on one or two points, especially with reference to discoveries in quantum mechanics.

Now, what is this quantum mechanics? What is new about its modern discovery? Previously, it was believed that atoms, being the ultimate constituents of this world, are all indivisible material particles, indivisible, static, inert material particles. However, the modern view is that the atom has an enormous complexity of structure. Even the simplest of atoms, the hydrogen atom, has this enormous complexity of structure, and it is a mode of expression of energy, not just inert. It is energy embodied. Every so-called passive, inert particle of matter is an embodiment of energy.

When we analyze the internal structure of the energy of an atom, we find there that it really resembles in its inner constitution the structure of the solar system in which we live. It is a solar system in miniature. Because just as in the solar system, the sun is in the center and the planets move, revolve around it. In the same way, when we look at the internal structure of an atom, at the center of the atom we find a positive nucleus which is the seemingly static center, and around that positive nucleus negative charges of electricity (electrons) revolve with great velocity. So this is the structure of an atom. But this is not the end of the story.

The further complexity is that the electrons have different orbits. There are different layers like in everything there are levels. Everything that exists in life has a multi-level structure, enormously complex. It has a hierarchical structure, higher and higher. In older physics, the hierarchy was not accepted. Everything was flat. But now there is another revolutionary discovery in science, the hierarchical structure of reality. Everything has a hierarchical structure. This is very evident in the human structure. This hierarchical structure has come to a very concentrated expression in man. That is why we have this erect posture expressing this hierarchy. All these energy centers are present in us, expressing the hierarchy of consciousness.

Reconciling Freedom and Determinism

Within the constitution of an atom there is this multi-level structure. And what do we find there? It has been discovered that this little electron, which revolves around the proton, mysteriously enough seems to have a life of its own. It has individuality. It has freedom. So, this is what I want you to understand: that even this little electron, which is a material thing, a negative charge of electricity, seems to have an intrinsic life and individuality of its own. It has freedom, baffling the calculations of the scientists who believed in the universality of causal determinism, everything is determined mechanically. The electron has defeated that theory.

The movement of the electron has demonstrated the freedom of its own to jump from one orbit to another orbit. This is very amazing that this little energy unit seems to have freedom of movement and can jump from one orbit to another orbit. This is called a quantum jump. And nobody has yet been able to figure out how this jump takes place. It cannot be figured out or calculated according to any known law of science. So you see, this opens up a whole new vista of thought: that if this freedom is possessed even by little electrons, how can we say that we human beings who stand at the apex of the ladder of evolution so far, who can dare say that we don't have freedom, that we are subject to just mechanical forces? Even a little atom is refuting that theory.

This is the first point I want to emphasize: that even from the standpoint of science and on the basis of scientific theory, in perfect harmony with known scientific knowledge, we can affirm the genuine authentic freedom of human beings. So, this can be accepted as a scientific truth. Now, the question of course would arise that if man has this freedom, or the electron has this freedom, then what about this law of causality, of cause and effect? For some time after this discovery there was some bewilderment and confusion. How can we reconcile these two things? On the one hand, we believe in the law of cause and effect and absolute determinism. On the other hand, we see there are sparks of freedom everywhere, in all the things of the world, from the minutest, infinitesimal atom to man. So, how do you reconcile these two things?

You know, we create many of our human problems. Many of our problems are problems of ignorance, self-created and artificially generated. So, the solution comes when that ignorance vanishes. We have created this problem when we say: how can there be both? The answer is: why not? Who tells us that there cannot be both? You see, we think that there cannot be both because we are still under the unconscious influence of the old Aristotelian law that A cannot be B *and* not B, which is another ignorance. But life is all the time knocking us out of that belief trying to teach us a lesson that A *can* be both B and not B. The same human being for example can be both mortal and immortal. He can be determined and free. This is what the true law is. It is called the law of polarity, the law of identity of opposites, which is a new discovery again in science, psychology, and philosophy today. When you come to examine the flesh and blood reality, it is a standing refutation of the old idea that A cannot be both B and not B. Everywhere in the concrete texture of reality, you will see the meeting of opposites without which nothing clicks, nothing takes place, nothing happens in life. Nothing is produced and created without the union of opposites.

Let me go back to that point where I said there can be both freedom and determinism. How do we explain that? If you are patient with me, I would like to say a few words to try to explain, to throw some light on this very important truth: the meeting of opposites. The following is from *The Rhythm of Truth*:

> Reality is two in one, one is two —
> Timeless eternity and ceaseless flux of time,
> Nameless mystery and nature's creative flow.
> The two are no separate spheres of Being.
> The formless bursts forth in endless forms.
> The nameless one reveals countless names.
> The spaceless reality expands in boundless space,
> And the timeless Spirit in endless time.

Everything operates in a system. The electron is operating not by itself, but within a system, the atomic system. We are operating in the social system. Every one of us lives in a social field, in a social organism, let me say. None of us lives by himself. Everything works within a system and exercises its freedom within that system. So, both of these are there. First of all, there is freedom. But then again, that freedom is not absolute freedom. For the electron there are certain orbits, and there is an energy field of the atom. The freedom of the electron is controlled by the limitation of that system. So this freedom of movement is not absolute. It is a relative freedom. So, the electron has both freedom and also limitation or determination.

Let me now give illustrations from our human life. We are right here a system. The Cultural Integration Fellowship is a system, an organization with members of this system. So, with regard to the different members of this organization, we can say that they have freedom and also some limitation. They have some uniform pattern of behavior which they accept, but also they have their freedom, both freedom and determination. In science this is called micro-freedom with macro-determination. You see, the electron's freedom is micro-freedom, little freedom. But that freedom is circumscribed within the macro-determination of the atom as a whole, which has its own behavior pattern, which is not disturbed by the movement of the electron. That determination imposes a limit on that electron, however free it may be. In the same way, each member of Cultural Integration Fellowship has his own freedom. For example, in his political life he may be a Republican, or a Democrat, or a Socialist, or a member of the Communist Party. That is not the business of the Fellowship. Each member is free to choose his own political affiliation as well as many other things in his private life. And it is not proper for the organization to interfere in the freedom of the individual member in all the different areas of life. But then again, the organization has some uniform pattern of behavior, some constitution, some bylaws. And this is not affected by the freedom of the members in other areas. There is perfect harmony between this free movement of the individual members and also the structural idiosyncrasy of the organization. To sum it up, I may say that there is no conflict between micro-freedom and macro-determination. This is how the distinction has been developed in the systems of view of modern science. In our lives, both freedom and necessity are there.

The Two Become One

Finally, let me now develop the whole thing into a further conclusion, and that is this: when in the course of our spiritual growth, we eventually reach the glorious height of self-realization or God-realization, what happens there? What happens at that moment? We find that at that height, there is a perfect unity of opposites, of freedom and necessity. The two become one. Instead of opposites being apart and separate from each other, the more you advance in life, the more you find that opposites become one.

When, for example, you attain enlightenment, you attain the full flowering of your potential. In nirvanic vision of truth, these opposites become one in your life. On one hand, you feel necessity, you feel oneness with the spirit of the whole, with the voice of eternity, or whatever expression you care to use. That is the greatest necessity that you can experience in life, the necessity of oneness with the spirit. That becomes the major source of inspiration in your life so that you begin to think and act and live out of that tremendous inward necessity of oneness with the whole. There is no taking away from that. This is what the German philosopher Immanuel Kant called the categorical imperative of the spirit. When you hear the voice of God, that becomes the supreme necessity of your life that becomes the categorical imperative of your life. It is an unconditional imperative of the light of truth that has dawned upon your mind. So that is necessity. But at the same time it is that very necessity which also constitutes your greatest freedom. Immediately you experience freedom.

Why? Because when you become one with the divine will, or one with cosmic consciousness, you realize that is your true self that is the Self of your self, the inmost center of your be-ing. And therefore, to be united with that means your highest freedom because you have found the true necessity at the center of your being. When you reach the highest level of your con-sciousness, the two things which seem to be so different in your life now become completely one. This is what the great psy-chologist Carl Jung meant when he said that on a higher level of consciousness the opposites become united. You discover the real unity of opposites in life and that is your great wisdom. Now, I shall just mention another point and I shall finish.

Another point in quantum mechanics is what is called criti-cal point. In the growth process when the critical moment aris-es, there is a jump, a quantum jump. This is another important thing. Suppose you put your kettle of water on the heat. It gets warmer and warmer. Up to a certain point this heating of the water doesn't produce any qualitative change. It is just getting warmer, that's all. There is no qualitative change, only quanti-tative change, change of degree, that's all. But then comes the critical point, the critical moment. And when the critical point comes, suddenly there is a qualitative change, transformation of quality. When water is suddenly qualitatively transformed into steam and then it hisses forth, it refuses to stay confined in that kettle any more. On the arrival of the critical point this water suddenly undergoes a metamorphosis of quality—a radi-cal, qualitative change from one thing into another. So, water now becomes steam, and steam has an opposite characteristic of water. Water goes down and steam goes up. Suddenly at that critical moment, water is metamorphosed, which means qualita-tively changed into an entirely different thing — steam. This is a miracle. It is the same kind of miracle, which happens in our life, which is called a spiritual miracle. This is called conversion of consciousness.

We have been evolving and growing little by little for a period of time. It is just quantitative change. A little more today, tomorrow you know a little more, day after tomorrow still a quantitative change. Your knowledge is quantitatively changing. In the same way, you are a little better today in your emotional tone, in your behavior pattern; maybe tomorrow a little better. These are all quantitative changes. But in the course of your inner growth and development, suddenly a critical moment arrives which is called the great psychological moment, the critical moment in the evolution of the evolving psyche. And as soon as that critical moment arrives, suddenly there is a new experience of illumination, a conversion of consciousness, a profound and moving inspiring spiritual experience, by whatever name you call it: Self-realization, God-realization, Being-realization, cosmic consciousness. What has happened is that in the course of your inner evolution, you have arrived now at a very critical moment when a qualitative change takes place within you, a radical transformation of your personality into the soaring flame of illumination, uniting you with the Supreme Being or with the Higher Self. So, this is the meaning of the saying in Buddhism that illumination or *satori* comes suddenly. But, behind this abrupt happening there is a slow continuous process of growth and evolution.

So, we understand now that just as there are quantum jumps in the atom on the part of the electron, so in the course of our development there are many quantum jumps. In meditation we experience these quantum jumps, jumps of consciousness or the unity of consciousness within you to other levels, from one level to another. In meditation you can feel these jumps. So this is really a fascinating mystery of the process of evolution. But if you understand the inner dynamics of this evolutionary process, you will no longer be confused by the fact that in the course of our development more and more of what have appeared to be opposites before become unified — opening up a whole new dimension of consciousness and experience.

Brain Research

In neurophysiology and brain research, some momentous discoveries have been made in recent times. One astounding discovery is that man has virtually two minds. This is perfectly in harmony with his two arms, two legs, two eyes, two ears, two nostrils, and so on. All action, all movement, all knowledge is the result of integrated functioning of two opposite yet cerebral organs. All this is in perfect keeping with the polarized structure of energy.

Man's two minds under the one skull are his two cerebral hemispheres or temporal lobes. Each of these two hemispheres, has its own highly specialized and distinguishable features and mode of functioning. This has been established on the evidence of a vast accumulation of experimental data obtained by electrical stimulation of various parts of the brain with the aid of extremely sensitive micro-electrodes.

It has been found that the left hemisphere is largely the abode of man's language ability, his distinctly human capacity for verbal communication and articulation of subtle distinctions of thought and nuances of meaning. It is the instrument of the rational, logical and analytic functions of the mind. It is specifically oriented to the world of space, time and evolution. The left-brain, which controls our extroverted actions, aims at survival and self-assertion. It is closely connected with such other portions of the brain as those which control the ever shifting feelings of pain and pleasure, sorrow and joy, and the impulses of fear and anger, worry and anxiety, aggression and domination. These are necessary for proper regulation of our need for adjustment in the outside world.

Closely interrelated with the left hemisphere is our right hand, which is especially skillful in manipulating things of the outside world. The right hand, controlled by the left temporal lobe is the organ par excellence of the extroverted mind oriented to nature's evolutionary goals of survival, success, and conquest of space. It specializes in expressing clear-cut ideas of the intellect whether through written language or through hand gestures. It is also especially adept in gaining manual skills and in managing masterly movement and self-expression.

On the other hand, the right hemisphere has been found to be the seat of intuitive knowledge, of esthetic, religious, and mystical experience. Man has intuitive apprehension of those features of reality which are not to be analyzed, but are to be grasped and appreciated in their wholeness. The right hemisphere has special proficiency in sustaining synthetic functions of the psyche, as well as transpersonal insights into the fathomless depth dimension of the timeless — the transcendental ground of the cosmic manifold. It controls our introverted movements of inward centering and upward ascending.

The right hemisphere is especially associated with the deep, sublime emotions of the heart. These include transcendental peace, or non-dual peace, which does not fluctuate. Pains and pleasures come with the changing circumstances of life. The right hemisphere is concerned with the unchanging reality behind the changing circumstances. It registers the unchanging emotions of unconditional love and the unconditional joy, which spring spontaneously from the depths of our being.

Most people have either the left hemisphere or the right hemisphere developed. There is a disproportion. They often do not function in unison, in harmony. Such things depend upon our cultivation. If we don't do that, even though there is something very precious there, it cannot be developed. These innate faculties gradually wither away for lack of exercise and become atrophied.

It has been rightly observed that in the unfoldment of the mainstream of Western culture, it is the intellect-ruled left-brain, which has on the whole played a predominant role. That is why among the fruits of Western civilization are to be counted the phenomenal growth of science and technology. In the unfoldment of the mainstream of Eastern culture, on the other hand, it is the intuition-ruled right hemisphere, which has on the whole played a dominant role. That is why among the treasures of the Eastern heritage are to be counted all the major religions of the world, the profundities of mystic vision, and priceless gems of original esthetic creation.

The highest cultural values of East and West can be harmonized in a higher synthesis. The emphasis in integral self-discipline is the dynamic integration of the two hemispheres. It is only through integrated functioning of both these sides that one can realize the fullness of human potential. The integrated functioning of our total being, including the synthesis of wisdom and compassion on the spiritual level, the synthesis of intellect and intuition on the mental level, and the synthesis of the right and left lobes of the brain on the physical level, are necessary for the creative wholeness of the individual man as an essential factor in the unitive wholeness of the human race.

IX

Beyond the Relaxation Response
by Herbert Benson and Marg Stark

Starting out in the profession of medicine in the United States more than thirty years ago, few questions would have struck me (Herbert Benson) as more irrelevant to science than the one posed by the title of this book, [*How Large Is God?* edited by John Templeton] After all, I was indoctrinated, as all Western physicians are in medical school and in my subsequent training, to believe that religion was the polar opposite of science. And it seemed to me, early in my career, that life's mysteries were, one by one, being explained by modern technology and research. So I became impressed with the enormity of science, not with the enormity of God. (When referring to God, the authors mean to describe all the deities that people believe in and worship.)[1]

In this posture, I was as wedded to conventional wisdom as my colleagues, all of us descendants of René Descartes, who, among others, forged the fissure between mind and body and between spirit and biology that prevails in Western scientific thought today. But as I began to practice medicine, I noticed that when it came to identifying sources of healing, my colleagues and I were often out of sync with patients. For so many of my patients, God and faith in God were not only relevant but real influences in their lives and in their health. Even so, I would not have ventured into a realm as unscientific as religion had it not been for mind/body research that led me to wonder if faith in God could be healing in and of itself.

Thus began my investigation into these largely unexplored resources, the resources on which patients relied every day of the year, sometimes consciously but often unconsciously, without the help of physicians or pharmaceuticals. My investigation meandered, as all scientific pursuits do, from experiment to research results, from new hypothesis to another experiment. But eventually, by way of science, I was compelled to look seriously at faith and at the magnitude of God as seen through the eyes of my patients.

The Calm Within

I came full circle and began to consider the influence faith in God could wield in the body, only after a prolonged scientific quest, the milestones of which I will now review. I was a young cardiologist when I received one of my first clues that something in the traditional approach to patient care was amiss. In those early years, I was troubled that by using a single test — the measurement of blood pressure — a physician would diagnose hypertension and prescribe a lifelong regimen of medicines with considerable side effects. However, before coming to see the doctor, the patient may have felt perfectly well and may not have experienced any other symptoms of serious illness. Hypertension, or sustained high blood pressure, is often symptomless but can have many detrimental, long-term effects, such as blocked arteries and enlarged and strained hearts, and can cause a variety of heart disorders and strokes.

Moreover, the readiness with which we physicians turned to prescription drugs bothered me. Not only were the side effects bothersome to patients but the medication often caused hypotension — blood pressure that is too low. This pattern suggested to me that patients' blood pressures may have been artificially elevated by the stress of visiting their physician. I thought that perhaps hypertension could be brought on by stressful events, a correlative that had not been fully recognized at that time.

To determine whether stress affected blood pressure, I began experimenting with monkeys in a Harvard Medical School laboratory and found that the monkeys, responding to certain incentives and disincentives, could actually learn to control their blood pressures. The monkeys required no medicines to increase or reduce the force of the blood that pumped through their arteries.

According to this study, stress could contribute to high blood pressure. And perhaps more important, this study made it seem possible that humans also could be trained to control and lower their blood pressure.

Transcendental Meditation

While the aforementioned experiments were underway, I was approached by some practitioners of Transcendental Meditation who believed that they were capable of lowering their blood pressures when they meditated. TM, as it was known, became popular in the late 1960s and early 1970s, under the leadership of Maharishi Mahesh Yogi. But I turned the TM practitioners away. My findings that stress might contribute to high blood pressure already had met with resistance at Harvard and elsewhere within the medical community, and I was fearful of jeopardizing my primate research by associating with what others deemed a "fringe organization."

But the TM practitioners were persistent, and eventually I brought some of them into the laboratory to measure physiologic changes that occurred while they engaged in meditation. Amazingly, the results proved them right. During their meditative exercises, they experienced low blood pressures, as well as significant reductions in heart rate, breathing rate, and speed of metabolism.

Ultimately, I called this physiologic calming effect "the relaxation response." Researchers before me already had discovered that this same kind of physical relaxation could be induced in animals. Nevertheless, the findings that TM could be used, as a willful exercise, to produce physiologic changes in humans sparked controversy in the medical community. While some of my colleagues were supportive, others urged me to abandon this line of research. Still others advised my superiors not to allow me to accept grants dedicated to this purpose, fearing the harm my association with a "cultish" element would do to Harvard's reputation.

In the end, it was Harvard's prestige and the open-mindedness of Dr. Robert H. Ebert, former dean of faculty of medicine at Harvard Medical School, who enabled my research to continue. The dean decided, "If Harvard can't take a chance, who can?" Thus, I was allowed to accept grants and to continue my studies of the relaxation response.

The Placebo Effect

One of the arguments used to dismiss the relaxation response was that it was "nothing but the placebo effect." The placebo effect describes a phenomenon in which a patient's beliefs and expectations about a pill or therapy contribute to the effectiveness of the treatment. Less well known is that a caregiver's beliefs and expectations, and the beliefs and expectations generated by the relationship between caregiver and patient, also contribute to the effectiveness of a pill or therapy.

Today, medicine primarily employs the placebo effect in new drug trials in which a control group is given inactive pills as a source of comparison with the medication being tested. But the theory behind the placebo effect that physicians have long recognized is that having faith in something makes a difference in medical outcomes. Traditionally, we have relied on the findings of Dr. Henry K. Beecher of Massachusetts General Hospital, reported in 1955, that the success rate of treating various types of illness with the placebo effect is roughly 30 percent.[2]

But when I looked closer, in an attempt to discredit the placebo's role in the bodily calm I had observed, I was instead impressed by how much more powerful and widely underrated the placebo effect was in medicine. My colleague Dr. David P. McCallie, Jr. and I looked at therapies used in the past to treat angina pectoris, pain that people with reduced blood flow to their heart muscles experience in their chest and arms. All the treatments have since been disproved and abandoned, and many of them, from injections of snake venom to the removal of the thyroid, sound downright absurd to modern ears.

And yet, Dr. McCallie and I found that when the treatments were in vogue, and were *believed in,* these physiologically indefensible and inherently worthless therapies for angina were effective 70 to 90 percent of the time. As these same treatments gradually fell out of favor and as physicians began to question their use, the effectiveness of the procedures indeed dropped to 30 to 40 percent. When patients and their doctors *had faith in* the therapies, the success rate in alleviating angina was two to three times the rate that Dr. Beecher attributed to the placebo effect.

As medical research amassed evidence that the mind and the body were interrelated, and as the mechanisms responsible for the placebo effect became clearer to me I renamed the effect "remembered wellness." Not only did remembered wellness better describe the brain's influence over physiology but I hoped that a new name would help medicine think about the phenomenon differently. After all, the placebo effect had become a pejorative, like "the dummy pill" and "it's all in your head," terms that doctors used to dismiss a patient's beliefs or emotions.

Dr. McCallie and I concluded that medicine seriously devalued remembered wellness as a therapeutic tool. But it took more than twenty years for the message of faith's *real* influence to find an audience in the medical community. In the meantime, I returned to elucidating the relaxation response, the study of which eventually led me back to the powers of remembered wellness.

The Relaxation Response

The next step in establishing the existence of the relaxation response was to explore whether TM alone could produce these physiologic changes, or whether other techniques could be used to elicit the relaxation response. TM involved two basic steps that were neither complicated nor mysterious. First, a person had to focus his or her mind on a word, phrase, or sound and to passively disregard interfering thoughts and return to the focus.

After three to five minutes of this repetitive mental focus, the relaxation response and its corresponding reductions in heart rate, breathing rate, rate of metabolism, and blood pressure occurred. Soon thereafter, I found that anyone who employed these two steps could elicit the physical changes of the relaxation response.

My colleagues and I, working first at Beth Israel Hospital in Boston, and later at the Deaconess Hospital where I helped establish Harvard's Mind/Body Medical Institute, discovered that not only was the relaxation response good for people in the short-term but it also had magnificent long-term preventive and restorative properties for people who elicited it regularly. In addition to hypertension, we found that the relaxation response either cured or lessened the effects of chronic pain, insomnia, infertility, premenstrual syndrome, anxiety and mild depression, headaches, and low self-esteem. The relaxation response also successfully reduced the nausea associated with chemotherapy, the pain and anxiety associated with surgery and X-ray procedures, and the frequency of cardiac arrhythmias in heart patients. And demonstrating its economic value, the elicitation of the relaxation response along with other stress-management techniques reduced the number of visits patients made to doctors and improved worker attendance on the job.

The relaxation response seemed to cure or help any medical condition or illness to the extent that condition or illness was caused or exacerbated by stress. Because this physiologic state of calm was accessible to everyone, I became convinced that the relaxation response was the opposite of, and perhaps the antidote for, the stress-induced fight-or-flight response.

Identified by Dr. Walter B. Cannon, the fight-or-flight response is the body's mobilization for either battle or escape, crucial to the survival of our distant ancestors and remaining a part of our genetic equipment today.[3] The physiologic changes that occur in the fight-or-flight response, namely heightened blood pressure, heart rate, breathing rate, and an increased metabolic rate, are precisely the opposite of those that occur during the relaxation response.

Even though we inherited the fight-or-flight response because it was good for our ancestors, it is not necessarily as good
for us in modern life. We do not usually expend the physical
energy that may be called forth in us when we are threatened.
Unlike cave men and women, our everyday threats are not usually physical. And the long-term effects of the repeated trigger-
ing of the stress-induced fight-or-flight response are injurious
to our bodies.

On the other hand, the relaxation response could restore a
body's equilibrium, offsetting the long-term damage that repeated stress and the fight-or-flight episodes caused. Although
our genetic heritage, indeed our wiring, often makes stress a
negative influence in our bodies in modern life, we also are
"wired" to experience the physical balm that my colleagues and
I had proven was healthy.

The Historical Perspective

To see whether or not the relaxation response had served this
purpose for ancient humans, I set about looking for historical
evidence of its presence. After two years of studying the literature of the world, I was thrilled to find that in every time, and in
every culture in recorded history, there were examples in which
humans described calming techniques. These methods incorpo-
rated the two essential steps — a repetitive mental focus and
passively ignoring any interrupting thoughts to return to one's
focus — and were indeed practiced in every religion, and sometimes outside of religion, in every nationality known to us.

I was pondering all this, some thirty years ago, as I mulled
over the wealth of documentation I had accumulated about the
relaxation response's physical value. I thought about how people in different cultures and times described the same physical
relaxation that I had observed in my patients' experiences. And
I considered what it meant that we were wired to experience this
physical balm, accessible by mental focusing.

Suddenly, I came to a startling conclusion: This is prayer!
The quiet ritual that people had observed in many different

ways in many different lands, and that religious leaders always said was good for people, seemed to call forth a particular set of bodily changes, opposite of those called upon in a crisis. People seemed to internalize and embody the repercussions of a repetitive form of prayer in ways that nourished them and promoted their physical health, not just their emotional and spiritual well-being.

The Study of Prayer

As true as this realization seemed to me, it was a conclusion I came to dread. Because, aside from being controversial, the study of prayer or any religious subject was considered unscientific. Nothing in my training as a physician prepared me to measure the effects God, or gods, had on my patients. As undeniable as it was that people throughout history had practiced and physically reacted to repetitive prayer in ways that I could prove were beneficial to the body, there was little or no scientific precedent for studying faith in God or religious traditions as healing methods.

Equally, I feared the reaction of the religious community. Would it appear to believers that I was trying to quantify God and to reduce the effects of religious faith to what I could see under a microscope? With this in mind, I went to see the dean of Harvard's Divinity School, Dr. Krister Stendhal. Dean Stendhal was a tall man, especially to me, as I am five-foot nine, even with my best posture. But his presence was bigger still, or so it seemed to me as I reviewed the points I had rehearsed.

I told him about the relaxation response and about the common experience of calm brought on by repetitive prayer as documented throughout history. I told him that in the process of distinguishing the relaxation response from the placebo effect, I had been impressed by the role belief and faith played in physical processes, a role misunderstood and underappreciated by modern medicine. And I told him I wanted to study the role of prayer, and specifically the mental focusing aspects of prayer, as well as the influence of faith. But I was worried about the effect my scientific study would have on believers and on the steadfastness of their faith.

Dean Stendhal listened closely to everything I said before he rose to deliver a reply. Looming above me, as I sank deeper into my chair's soft cushions, Dean Stendhal answered my queries directly, "Young man, don't worry about us. Religion and prayer were here before you and they will be there after you. You do your thing and we will do ours."

Spirituality Linked to Health Benefits

So it was that I began the delicate study of repetitive prayer, of the faith in God that usually accompanied it, and of the extent to which both helped people in measurable, medical ways. The effects of the relaxation response already had been established. Nonreligious people and those who approached mental focusing as a health-enhancing exercise, not as a spiritual one, experienced physiologic changes and benefits just as religious believers did.

But as much as traditional medicine urged me to exclude faith from consideration, 80 percent of my patients chose to say a prayer to elicit the calm of the relaxation response. Because my patients were naturally drawn to prayer, I found myself in the awkward position of being a physician who taught people to pray, despite the fact that I encouraged people to use any repetitive word, phrase, image, or even a repetitive activity, such as knitting or jogging, to focus their minds and bodies. My only stipulation was that it be something that patients liked and felt comfortable with, so that they would be more apt to adhere to the routine of eliciting the relaxation response.

Not only did most patients choose scriptures or prayers but 25 percent of those who elicited the relaxation response experienced an increase in spirituality, whether or not they intended to. Dr. Jared D. Kass, a professor at Lesley College Graduate School of Arts and Sciences in Cambridge, Massachusetts, other colleagues, and I developed a questionnaire to pin down what people meant by "spiritual" when they talked about the effects of mental focusing. Again, whether or not the practitioners considered themselves religious, those surveyed said two things about this sense of spirituality: They felt the presence of an energy, a force, a power — God — that was beyond themselves, and this presence felt close to them.

In addition, the 25 percent who felt more spiritual as the result of eliciting the relaxation response experienced fewer medical symptoms than those who did not experience spirituality. This amorphous sense that we had nailed down — the presence of something beyond them that nevertheless felt close to them — seemed to lend their bodies additional healing effects, over and above those of the relaxation response.

FOOTNOTES:

[1]   Herbert Benson with Marg Stark, *Timeless healing: The Power and Biology of Belief* (New York: Scribner, 1996) pp. 1-350.

[2]   Henry K. Beecher, "The Powerful Placebo," *Journal of the American Medical Association* 159 (1995): 1602-1606.

[3]   Walter B. Cannon, *The Way of an Investigator: A Scientist's Experience in Medical Research* (New York: W.W. Norton, 1945).

X

On Creationism
by Tom Harpur

[This article appeared in *The Toronto Star*, February 20, 2005]

From a page of letters in *The New York Times* (Jan. 24) to the *Star's* recent feature on the topic — *"E" word makes U.S. teachers skittish* (Feb. 5) — it's more than obvious that a battle everybody thought had been ended several times in the past is still being waged. In fact, it's heating up on a far wider front than anyone could have dreamed of a decade ago.

The bitter, divisive issue in thousands of schools across the U.S. today is the teaching of evolution in biology classes. Fundamentalist Christians are demanding that "intelligent design," which is really their new mantra for "creationism," be given equal billing in high school science classrooms.

For them, Darwinism is synonymous with teaching atheism and so they are insisting that at the very least evolution disclaimers should be added to science curricula. They insist evolution is "just a theory" — one among many. Given that the U.S. President himself has said publicly "the jury is still out on that one" — that is, whether evolution or creationism is right — you can't blame those who espouse the same simple theology as he does for their present militancy.

In many ways, though, it's a sad commentary on the state of religion in the U.S. and on the general level of understanding of the majority of Christians there. Evolution is not "just a theory" if by that is meant it's merely a fragile, unproven idea likely to be revoked at any moment in favor of something else.

In science, a theory of this magnitude and potency — in terms of the vast mass of data, which it alone clearly explains — has become a reliable, trusted model. Yes, it can be altered in details; yes, it is always subject to further testing, and, yes, it has its gaps. But no credible scientist today questions its overall validity.

Creationism, together with its creed of a "young Earth" and "instant humans" in Eden, is soundly refuted by the fossil records alone, and ongoing attempts by creationists to argue down evolutionists are painfully damaging to Christianity in general.

The tragedy is that this furor is utterly unnecessary and a hugely wasteful spending of moral and material energies in a bogus campaign. Moral challenges such as child poverty, excessive spending by the military, space weapons planning, and a host of other matters calling for spiritual outrage and action, are neglected instead.

When will these conservative religionists wake up and realize you don't have to choose between the best that science can offer, that is, evolution, and a lively belief in a divine Mind or God behind the origins and development of life?

Looking in the Bible for a scientific account of origins is like looking in the phone directory for a recipe for angel cake.

Science begins with curiosity and deals with the "what and how" of things in the universe; religion flows from awe and wonder and tries to deal with the ultimate question: Why? Why are we here at all? The answers are wholly compatible. That God used the method of evolution to select the myriad species of Earth is much more "miraculous" than some kind of magical fiat in a mythical Garden of Eden. The "Big Bang" is a greater miracle than any described in Genesis.

Most sophisticated, religious persons find no conflict whatever between science and faith. Some of the greatest scientists of our era have been or are deeply religious (though often unorthodox in outlook.) For example, Albert Einstein was able to say: "I maintain that the cosmic religious feeling is the strongest and noblest motive for scientific research."

It's important to understand why the fundamentalists are so fired up on all this. The reasons go far beyond their misunderstanding that evolution and belief in God cannot peacefully co-exist.

To begin, their doctrine of an infallible, inerrant Bible, to be taken literally unless the context indicates otherwise, is threatened if science says we are the product of millions of years of natural selection while Genesis talks as though humans snapped to attention fully formed about 6,000 years ago. Inability to distinguish myth from history presents them with this false dilemma.

But, their difficulties increase exponentially. If there was no age of innocence in a historic Eden, if there has been an upward moving process involving hundreds of millions, even billions of years, then there was no literal, primal "fall" involving "original sin." With this, the whole edifice begins to shake. No "Fall" means no monumental problem of sin staining everything human. No "Fall" means no cosmic necessity for a Redeemer, no Cross of Atonement, no bloody Passion. The evangelical "plan of salvation" totters and collapses.

It doesn't make much sense anyway, but evolution administers the *coup de grace*. This means bad news for the good news. What's feared most of all is this call to change.

XI

The Dynamic Universe
by Fritjof Capra

The more one studies the religious and philosophical texts of the Hindus, Buddhists, and Taoists, the more it becomes apparent that in all of them the world is conceived in terms of movement, flow, and change. This dynamic quality of Eastern philosophy seems to be one of its most important features. The Eastern mystics see the universe as an inseparable web, whose interconnections are dynamic and not static. The cosmic web is alive; it moves, grows, and changes continually. Modern physics, too, has come to conceive of the universe as such a web of relations and, like Eastern mysticism, has recognized that this web is intrinsically dynamic. The dynamic aspect of matter arises in quantum theory as a consequence of the wave-nature of subatomic particles, and is even more essential in relativity theory, as we shall see, where the unification of space and time implies that the being of matter cannot be separated from its activity. The properties of subatomic particles can therefore only be understood in a dynamic context; in terms of movement, interaction, and transformation.

According to quantum theory, particles are also waves, and this implies that they behave in a very peculiar way. Whenever a subatomic particle is confined to a small region of space, it reacts to this confinement by moving around. The smaller the region of confinement, the faster will the particle "jiggle" around in it. This behavior is a typical "quantum effect," a feature of the subatomic world which has no macroscopic analogy. To see how it comes about, we have to remember that particles are represented, in quantum theory, by wave packets. The length of such a wave packet represents the uncertainty in the location of the particle. The following wave pattern, for example, corresponds to a particle located somewhere in the region X;

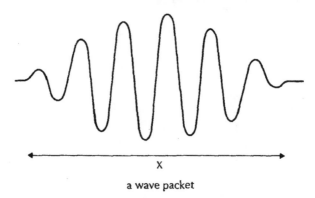

X

a wave packet

where exactly we cannot say with certainty. If we want to localize the particle more precisely, that is, if we want to confine it to a smaller region, we have to squeeze its wave packet into this region (see diagram below). This, however, will affect the wavelength of the wave packet, and consequently the velocity of the particle. As a result, the particle will move around; the more it is confined, the faster it will move.

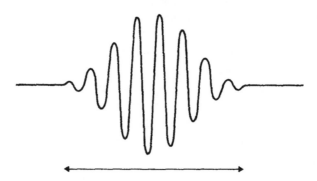

squeezing the wave packet into a smaller region

The tendency of particles to react to confinement with motion implies a fundamental "restlessness" of matter which is characteristic of the subatomic world. In this world, most of the material particles are bound to the molecular, atomic, and nuclear structures, and therefore are not at rest but have an inherent tendency to move out — they are intrinsically restless. According to quantum theory, matter is thus never quiescent, but always in a state of motion. Macroscopically, the material objects around us may seem passive and inert, but when we magnify such a "dead" piece of stone or metal, we see that it is full of activity. The closer we look at it, the more alive it appears. All the material objects in our environment are made of atoms which link up with each other in various ways to form an enormous variety of molecular structures which are not rigid and motionless, but oscillate according to their temperature and in harmony with the thermal vibrations of their environment. In the vibrating atoms, the electrons are bound to the atomic nuclei by electric forces which try to keep them as close as possible, and they respond to this confinement by whirling around extremely fast. In the nuclei, finally, the protons and neutrons are pressed into minute volume by the strong nuclear forces, and consequently race about with unimaginable velocities.

Modern physics, then, pictures matter not at all as passive and inert, but as being in a continuous dancing and vibrating motion whose rhythmic patterns are determined by the molecular, atomic and nuclear structures. This is also the way in which the Eastern mystics see the material world. They all emphasize that the universe has to be grasped dynamically, as it moves, vibrates and dances; that nature is not in a static, but a dynamic equilibrium. In the words of a Taoist text:

> The stillness in stillness is not the real stillness. Only when there is stillness in movement can the spiritual rhythm appear which pervades heaven and earth.[1]

In physics, we recognize the dynamic nature of the universe not only when we go to small dimensions — to the world of atoms and nuclei — but also when we turn to large dimensions — to the world of stars and galaxies.

Through our powerful telescopes we observe a universe in ceaseless motion. Rotating clouds of hydrogen gas contract to form stars, heating up in the process until they become burning fires in the sky. When they have reached that stage, they still continue to rotate, some of them ejecting material into space which spirals outwards and condenses into planets circling around the star. Eventually, after millions of years, when most of its hydrogen fuel is used up, a star expands, and then contracts again in the final gravitational collapse. This collapse may involve gigantic explosions, and may even turn the star into a black hole. All these activities — the formation of stars out of interstellar gas clouds, their contraction and subsequent expansion, and their final collapse — can actually be observed somewhere in the skies.

The spinning, contracting, expanding or exploding stars cluster into galaxies of various shapes — flat discs, spheres, spirals, and so on — which, again, are not motionless but rotate. Our galaxy, the Milky Way, is an immense disc of stars and gas turning in space like a huge wheel, so that all its stars — including the sun and its planets — move around the galaxy's center. The universe is, in fact, full of galaxies strewn through all the space we can see; all spinning like our own.

When we study the universe as a whole, with its millions of galaxies, we have reached the largest scale of space and time; and again, at that cosmic level, we discover that the universe is not static — it is expanding! This has been one of the most important discoveries in modern astronomy. A detailed analysis of the light received from distant galaxies has shown that the whole swarm of galaxies expands, and that it does so in a well-orchestrated way; the recession velocity of any galaxy we observe is proportional to the galaxy's distance. The more distant the galaxy, the faster it moves away from us; at double the distance, the recession velocity will also double. This is true not only for distances measured from our galaxy, but applies to any point of reference. Whichever galaxy you happen to be in, you will observe the other galaxies rushing away from you; nearby galaxies at several thousand miles per second, farther ones at higher speeds, and the farthest at velocities approaching the speed of light. The light from galaxies beyond that distance will never reach us, because they move away from us faster than the speed of light. Their light is — in the words of Sir Arthur Eddington — "like a runner on an expanding track with the winning post receding faster than he can run."

Expansion in a Higher Dimension

To have a better idea of the way in which the universe expands, we have to remember that the proper framework for studying its large-scale features is Einstein's general theory of relativity. According to this theory, space is not "flat," but is "curved," and the precise way in which it is curved is related to the distribution of matter by Einstein's field equations. These equations can be used to determine the structure of the universe as a whole; they are the starting point of modern cosmology.

When we talk about an expanding universe in the framework of general relativity, we mean an expansion in a higher dimension. Like the concept of curved space, we can only visualize such a concept with the help of a two-dimensional analogy.

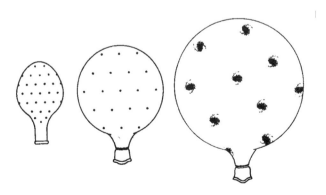

Imagine a balloon with a large number of dots on its surface. The balloon represents the universe, its two-dimensional curved surface representing the three-dimensional curved space, and the dots on the surface the galaxies in that space. When the balloon is blown up, all the distances between the dots increase. Whichever dot you choose to sit on, all the other dots will move away from you. The universe expands in the same way: whichever galaxy an observer happens to be in, the other galaxies will all move away from him.

An obvious question to be asked about the expanding universe is: how did it all start? From the relation between the distance of a galaxy and its recession velocity — which is known as Hubble's law — one can calculate the starting point of the expansion, in other words, the age of the universe. Assuming that there has been no change in the rate of expansion, which is by no means certain, one arrives at an age of the order of 10,000 million years. This, then, is the age of the universe. Most cosmologists believe today that the universe came into being in a highly dramatic event about 10,000 million years ago, when its total mass exploded out of a small primeval fireball. The present expansion of the universe is seen as the remaining thrust of this initial explosion. According to this "big-bang" model, the moment of the big bang marked the beginning of the universe and the beginning of space and time. If we want to know what happened before that moment, we run — again — into severe difficulties of thought and language. In the words of Sir Bernard Lovell:

> There we reach the great barrier of thought because we begin to struggle with the concepts of time and space before they existed in terms of our everyday experience. I feel as though I've suddenly driven into a great fog barrier where the familiar world has disappeared. [2]

As far as the future of the expanding universe is concerned, Einstein's equations do not provide a unique answer. They allow for several different solutions corresponding to different models of the universe. Some models predict that the expansion will continue forever; according to others, it is slowing down and will eventually change into a contraction. These models describe an oscillating universe, expanding for billions of years, then contracting until its total mass has condensed into a small ball of matter, then expanding again, and so on without end.

This idea of a periodically expanding and contracting universe, which involves a scale of time and space of vast proportions, has arisen not only in modern cosmology, but also in ancient Indian mythology. Experiencing the universe as an organic and rhythmically moving cosmos, the Hindus were able to develop evolutionary cosmologies, which come very close to our modern scientific models. One of these cosmologies is based on the Hindu myth of *līlā* — the divine play — in which *Brahman* transforms himself into the world. *Līlā* is a rhythmic play, which goes on in endless cycles, the One becoming the many, and the many returning into the One. In the *Bhagavad Gītā*, the god Krishna describes this rhythmic play of creation in the following words:

> At the end of the night of time all things return to my nature; and when the new day of time begins I bring them again into light.

> Thus through my nature I bring forth all creation and this rolls around in the circles of time.

> But I am not bound by this vast work of creation. I am and I watch the drama of works.

> I watch and in its work of creation nature brings forth all that moves and moves not: and thus the revolutions of the world go round. [3]

The Hindu sages were not afraid to identify this rhythmic divine play with the evolution of the cosmos as a whole. They pictured the universe as periodically expanding and contracting and gave the name *kalpa* to the unimaginable time span between the beginning and the end of one creation. The scale of this ancient myth is indeed staggering; it has taken the human mind more than two thousand years to come up again with a similar concept.

FOOTNOTES:

1   *Ts'ai-ken t'an*: quoted in T. Leggett, *A First Zen Reader*, p. 229, and in N.W. Ross, *Three Ways of Asian Wisdom*, p. 144.
2   A.C.B. Lovell, *The Individual and the Universe*, p. 93.
3   *Bhagavad Gītā*, 9.7-10.

XII

On Evolution
by Swami Chinmayananda

The modern materialist who denounces religion and claims to be an atheist probably does not know that the super structure of his skepticism is built upon the sands of eighteenth-century materialism. In the eighteenth century, scientists discovered that matter was composed of mere physical units called "atoms." They claimed that a combination of atoms constituted molecules and that molecules packed together formed a substance. To them, therefore, the concept of a God or a Creative Power behind all names and forms seemed absurd and redundant. In that age of materialism, the biologist-prophet, Darwin, was the seer and his theory of evolution gave a stimulus to the materialism advocated and demonstrated by physicists in their laboratories.

But this was in the eighteenth century. Today, the very skeptical West has discovered that the atom is further divisible and is, in content, nothing but energy. Though science has progressed to prove that energy is the fundamental factor in matter, a corresponding change in the view of the scriptures has yet to come about. Though people in the West claim to be progressive and scientific-minded, they are, in fact, conservative and closed-minded. If they were to readjust their view of life, according to the new discoveries in the laboratories, they would certainly turn more of their attention towards the spiritualization of their lives. Indeed, for any society where the scientific spirit predominates, Vedanta is bound to prove to be the most satisfying religion.

SWAMI CHINMAYANANDA

The Measuring Rod of Evolution

According to Darwin's theory, evolution is measured in terms of the development of the physiological equipment and the level of mind and intelligence in the specimen. But for the Eastern philosophers, while they accept different strata of beings, the measuring rod for the level of evolution is not the physical or mental development. It is *the amount of awareness, manifested in a thing or being.*

In stone life there is a mere expression of existence, but no awareness or intelligence as such. A piece of rock does not seem to feel bothered by the kicks of a mule, nor does it exult because a king has chosen to dine over it! It is totally unaware of the external climatic conditions, the place or the treatment it receives. In the vegetable kingdom, however, we find a greater degree of awareness. A plant is aware of the external conditions of humidity or the conditions of the soil. When there is a dearth of moisture, the plants dry up. When water is supplied, they react to the external condition and absorbing the same, seem to smile with liveliness and charm.

Plants react to the seasons and their corresponding climatic conditions. During spring they bloom fully and joyously. Thus, the more sympathetically we observe mineral and vegetable life, the more we find to our complete satisfaction that there is a greater degree of awareness in plant life.

When plant life is compared to the animal kingdom, we find the latter manifests a yet greater degree of consciousness. An animal not only reacts to external circumstances but also seems to feel, perhaps only to a limited extent, the conditions of its own mind and intellect. Birds and animals feel an instinctive responsibility towards their young and display towards them a great amount of consideration, sympathy, tolerance, and love, at least for a short period. Birds and animals also prepare for themselves proper shelter for the changing climatic conditions. Birds and fishes living in the upper regions of the Ganges start moving down as winter approaches. Birds move into the higher valleys as summer sets in the plains. So too, we are told that in the jungle, wild animals migrate from place to place seeking better caves, safer dens, and healthier environments.

Of all beings, man seems to be most intensely aware of the external world and internal states of the mind. This intensity of consciousness is, again, perceptibly different from man to man. It is not all men that are at all times fully aware or conscious of all the external or internal life, but it is only a rare few that are the most sensitive, not only to their outer life, but also to the patterns of their thoughts, emotions, feelings and ideas.

Thus, to the ancient seers of our scriptures, the theory of evolution is a story of the slow unfoldment of consciousness through more and more complex and highly evolved equipment. It is the great Plan of Nature expressed from stone life to human life, the one continuous golden vein of growth and development running through all manifestations culminating in the complete unfoldment of Consciousness.

The seers were not mere scientists meddling with material equipment on an insignificant table in a corner of a laboratory. They were men of giant wisdom observing life as a whole, in the canvas of their own mind and intellect, to study the great theme of life, in a spirit of pure detachment. Even here, it is not life of a given period of history, but life in its totality gushing out through the channels of ages. Each master conditioned and trained his disciples for such a study of observed life and passed down his conclusions to them. They, in turn, observed all through their lives, their own generations, working through the same truths. It is the sum total of their unanimous conclusions that constitute the declarations of the Vedantic philosophy.

XIII

God Through Physics
by Sudhakar Raje

Atheists, agnostics, and rationalists reject God because He cannot be "proved" scientifically. Revelation of divinity, they say, is an intuitive phenomenon, and is not governed by the laws of physical science. But where is science heading? The dizzy progress made by science — by physics, of all sciences! — during the last fifty years makes one wonder if our ancient seers (*rishis*) who sought to "experience" divinity were not actually pointing the direction science would take thousands of years later. They called God Universal Consciousness (*Paramātmā*), and they based their quest for *Paramātmā* on the intuitive awareness that the visible/comprehensible reality surrounding us was in fact a mist of illusion hiding the "real reality" — *Brahma Satyam, Jagat Mithyā.*

Newtonian physics, two hundred years ago, had no patience with such duality. It conceived the Universe as a Great Machine, which was operable by definite laws of motion, gravity, and so on. "The Great Machine runs blindly on, and all things in it are but cogs." The premise of Newtonian physics was that the Universe is governed by laws that are susceptible to rational understanding.

But now the latest refinements of physics, like Particle Physics and Quantum Mechanics, definitely indicate that reality, "real" reality, is not confined within the limitations of rational understanding. On the opposite side our understanding of "apparent," is what we take to be true. The reality acceptable to us is empirical.

But with Bell's Theorem and Bohm's Theory the scientific concept of reality has taken what we may call a quantum leap. In 1964 J.S. Bell, a physicist at the European Organization for Nuclear Re-search (CERN) in Switzerland, published a mathematical paper known as Bell's Theorem. It implies that, at a deep and fundamental level, the "separate parts" of the universe are all connected in an intimate and immediate way. In short, Bell's Theorem, considered by some physicists as the most important single work, perhaps, in the history of physics, is very much compatible with the enlightened experience of universal unity — the all-permeating *Paramātmā*.

Quantum physicists had already realized in the 1920's that our commonsense ideas were inadequate for describing the behavior of subatomic particles. Bell's Theorem shows that commonsense ideas are inadequate even to describe macroscopic events of our everyday world. As Henry Stapp, a physicist at the Lawrence Berkeley Laboratory, wrote: "The important thing about Bell's Theorem is that it puts the dilemma posed by quantum phenomena clearly into the realm of macroscopic phenomena... (it) shows that our ordinary ideas about the world are somehow profoundly deficient even on the macroscopic level." This is another way of saying that subatomic reality and macroscopic-universal-reality are equally incomprehensible, or equal in being incomprehensible *–Yat piṇḍe tat Brahmāṇḍe*.

David Bohm, Professor of physics at Birbeck College, University of London, proposes that Quantum Physics is, in fact, based upon a perception of a new order. According to Bohm, "We must turn physics around. Instead of starting with parts and showing how they work together, we start with the whole." In other words, Quantum Physics depends upon the acceptance of the Universe as a unity — a unity that is succinctly revealed by Lord Krishna in the *Bhagavad Gītā* when He says everything emanates from Him and everything merges unto Him; He is the one source of all creation.

SUDHAKAR RAJE

Unbroken Wholeness

Bohm's Theory is compatible with Bell's Theorem. Bell's Theorem implies that the apparently "separate parts" of the Universe could be intimately connected at a deep and fundamental level. Bohm asserts that the most fundamental level is an "unbroken wholeness," which is, in his words, "that-which-is." Our *rishis* called it *Tat-tvam.*

Bohm's physics requires, in his words, a new "instrument of thought," — an instrument that would radically alter consciousness of the observer of reality, reorienting it towards a perception of the "unbroken wholeness" of which everything is a form, a manifestation. But for us in this country this is not as much of an obstacle as it appears to a Westerner. We have already conceived of a whole that remains a whole even after the whole is taken away from it —

> *Om pūrṇam adaḥ pūrṇam idaṁ,*
> *pūrṇāt pūrṇam udachyate,*
> *Pūrṇasya pūrṇam ādāya,*
> *pūrṇam eva avaśiṣyate.*
> *Om Śāntiḥ Śāntiḥ Śāntiḥ*

> That (*Brahman*) is Whole. This (apparent creation) is also Whole. From Wholeness (*Brahman*) this whole (apparent creation) becomes manifest. Bringing (out) this whole (apparent creation) from Wholeness, the Wholeness (*Brahman*) alone remains. Om Peace, Peace, Peace.

To quote Gary Zukav in his engrossing book, *The Dancing Wu Li Masters: An overview of the New Physics*, "There already exists an instrument of thought based upon an 'unbroken wholeness.' There exist a number of sophisticated psychologies/philosophies distilled from thousands of years of practice and introspection, whose sole purpose has been to develop this thought instrument." "These psychologies are what we commonly call 'Eastern Religions.' All Eastern Religions (psychologies) are compatible in a very fundamental way with Bohm's physics and philosophy. All of them are based upon the experience of a pure, undifferentiated reality which is that-which-is."

By "Eastern Religions" Zukav mainly means Hinduism and Buddhism, and says it "would be foolish to ignore" their similarities with Bohm's Physics. Then he quotes the following sentences by way of examples:

"The word 'reality' is derived from the roots 'thing' (*res*) and 'think' (*revi*). 'Reality' means 'everything you can think about.'"

"The ultimate perception does not originate in the brain or any material structure... The subtle mechanism of knowing the truth does not originate in the brain."

"There is a similarity between thought and matter."

"Taken out of context," writes Zukav, "there is no absolute way of knowing whether these statements were made by Professor Bohm or a Tibetan Buddhist. In fact these sentences were excerpted from two physics lectures that Professor Bohm gave at Berkeley in April 1977. ... Two of these three statements were taken from the second lecture, the one given to advanced physicists."

Beyond the Symbols

Hinduism — as every Eastern Religion — resorts to the use of symbols, but its function is to enable the mind to escape the confines of the symbolic.

According to this view, everything is a symbol, not only words and concepts, but also people and things. Beyond the confines of the symbolic lies that which is, pure awareness, the experience of the "suchness" of reality. No wonder although Bohm's theories are looked upon with some skepticism by many physicists, they would find an immediate sympathetic reception among thousands of people nurtured in Western materialism who have now turned their backs on science in a personal quest for the ultimate nature of reality. If, says Zukav, Bohm's physics became the main thrust of the Physics of the future, "Physics curricula of the twenty-first century could include classes in meditation." In other words physicists in the twenty-first century A.D. may well go back to what our seers and *rishis* were doing in the twenty-first century B.C. and far beyond.

The horizons of modern physics are rapidly expanding, and the modern physicist has replaced the rigidity of approach represented by Newtonian mechanics by extreme openness. Isidor Rabi, Nobel Prize winner and Chairman Emeritus of the Physics Department at Columbia University, wrote in 1975: "I don't think that physics will ever have an end. I think that the novelty of nature is such that its variety will be infinite — not just in changing forms but in the profundity of insight and the newness of ideas...." Stapp wrote in 1971: ".... human inquiry can continue indefinitely to yield important new truths." Physicists today accept that the physics of nature, like human experience itself, is infinitely diverse.

Hinduism — or Eastern Religion as such — may not have anything to say about physics, but it has a great deal to say about human experience. In forceful — albeit to a Hindu sensitivity rather outlandish — language Gary Zukav writes in *The End of Science*, the end chapter of his fascinating book, *The Dancing Wu Li Masters: An overview of the New Physics.*

> In Hindu mythology Kali, the Divine Mother, is the symbol of the infinite diversity of experience. Kali represents the entire physical plane. She is the drama, tragedy, humor, and sorrow of life. She is the brother, father, sister, mother, lover and friend. She is the fiend, monster, beast, and brute. She is the sun and the ocean. She is the grass and the dew. She is our sense of accomplishment and our sense of doing worthwhile. Our thrill of discovery is a pendant on her bracelet. Our gratification is a spot of color on her cheek. Our sense of importance is the bell on her toe. This full and seductive, terrible and wonderful earth mother always has something to offer. Hindus know the impossibility of seducing her or conquering her, and the futility of loving her or hating her. So they do the only thing they can do. They simply honor her.

Ancient intuition and modern research are perceptibly converging. Hoary Hinduism and up-to-date science appear definitely compatible. Twentieth century Physics has taken the first discernible steps towards God-realization. Will the twenty-first century Physics see the journey's end?

PART THREE

The Scientists Speak

*It is going to be crucial to have
a proper ethical viewpoint
guiding the uses of science.*
George F.R. Ellis

I maintain that the cosmic religious feeling is the strongest and noblest motive for scientific research. Only those who realize the immense efforts and, above all, the devotion without which pioneer work in theoretical science cannot be achieved are able to grasp the strength of the emotion out of which alone such work, remote as it is from the immediate realities of life, can issue. What a deep conviction of the rationality of the universe and what a yearning to understand, were it but a feeble reflection of the mind revealed in this world, Kepler and Newton must have had to enable them to spend years of solitary labor in disentangling the principles of celestial mechanics!

Those whose acquaintance with scientific research is derived chiefly from its practical results easily develop a completely false notion of the mentality of the men who, surrounded by a skeptical world, have shown the way to kindred spirits scattered wide through the world and the centuries. Only one who has devoted his life to similar ends can have a vivid realization of what has inspired these men and given them the strength to remain true to their purpose in spite of countless failures. It is cosmic religious feeling that gives a man such strength. A contemporary has said, not unjustly, that in this materialistic age of ours the serious workers are the only profoundly religious people.

Albert Einstein

XIV

Physicists and Spirituality
by Thomas J. McFarlane

In 1905, at age 26, Albert Einstein rocked the scientific world
with his special theory of relativity, showing time and space
to be dependent on the observer. His famous equation $E=mc^2$
revealed matter and energy as inter-changeable forms of the
same substance. Ten years later he devised the general theory
of relativity, explaining gravity not as a force but rather as the
warping of space-time. Before Einstein, physicists had viewed
time and space as completely separate from each other, matter and energy as fundamentally different, and gravitation as a
mysterious force that acted at a distance through empty space.
Einstein's work proved all these beliefs wrong, revolutionizing
basic concepts of reality.

Like many other pioneers of modern physics, Einstein taught
in German universities until the Nazis came to power. In 1933,
he fled to the United States and spent the rest of his active life
at Princeton University's Institute for Advanced Study in New
Jersey. There, he continued the search for a unified field theory
that would unite space, time and gravity with electromagnetism;
more years of his professional life were spent on this than any
other project.

Throughout his life, Einstein was concerned with philosophical as well as scientific questions. He was deeply concerned
with the human condition, social injustices, and virtues such as
selflessness and devotion to higher ideals. His religious views,
were largely influenced by the 17th-century philosopher Baruch

Spinoza, whose life paralleled Einstein's in many respects. Like Einstein's theories, Spinoza's greatest work, *Ethics*, expressed its rational mysticism behind logical abstractions while concluding that nature's harmony proves God's existence, and that elegant simplicity — the "oneness" Einstein had long hoped to find in the elusive unified field theory — holds the key to all understanding. As Einstein wrote, "All religions, arts and sciences are branches of the same tree. All these aspirations are directed toward ennobling man's life, lifting it from the sphere of mere physical existence and leading the individual toward freedom."

At the same time as Einstein was doing his early work, other physicists in Germany and other parts of Europe were beginning to probe the microscopic world of the atom. As they did, they found that the classical physical laws of mechanics, electrodynamics, and thermodynamics no longer fit the experimental data. They saw particles of matter behave like waves and waves of light behave like particles. Strict laws of cause and effect gave way to such spontaneous, unpredictable events as radioactive decay. And atoms, they discovered, only absorbed and emitted energy in discrete chunks, called quanta. This last feature gave its name to the system that finally explained it all: quantum theory.

Max Planck, a German physicist, had produced the earliest hints of quantum physics with his radiation formula, which first introduced the quantum principle into physics. A complete theoretical deduction of the formula showed classical notions of the atom to be flawed and laid the foundation for the work of Bohr and his colleagues in other parts of Europe and the United States.

Among them, the Danish physicist Niels Bohr played a central role in both the discovery and development of quantum theory. His correspondence principle showed the way to relate new quantum laws coherently to established laws of classical physics. Bohr's principle of complementarity allowed physicists to make sense of paradoxes such as the fact that subatomic particles had both wave and particle properties. Second only to Einstein among 20th-century physicists, the Danish scientist participated in a long-running scientific debate with Einstein over the significance of quantum theory. Einstein refused to accept that nature is fundamentally random and devised "thought experiments" to support his maxim that "God does not play dice with the universe," as Bohr's interpretation of quantum theory seemed to imply. In each instance, Bohr showed Einstein where he had gone wrong. He also likened modern physics to Eastern mysticism in these words: "For a parallel to the lesson of atomic theory, [we must turn] to those kinds of problems with which thinkers like the Buddha and Lao Tzu have been confronted, when trying to harmonize our position as spectators and actors in the great drama of existence."

Werner Heisenberg, one of Bohr's students, discovered the mathematical laws of quantum theory in 1925, and formulated the famous Heisenberg uncertainty principle in 1927. According to this principle, it is impossible to measure both the exact position and velocity of a particle at the same time. During World War II, Heisenberg remained in Germany as the head of Hitler's unsuccessful nuclear weapons program. He was interned in England after the war but eventually returned to Germany to continue his theoretical research as director of the Max Planck Institute. Heisenberg's philosophical views can best be described as a modern scientific form of Plato's rational mysticism. "The search for the 'one,' for the ultimate source of all understanding," he wrote, "has doubtless played a similar role in the origin of both religion and science."

Wolfgang Pauli, a young prodigy who worked as Bohr's assistant, is best known for the Pauli exclusion principle. Developed in 1925, the principle held that no two electrons in an atom, can have the same attributes. Although a brilliant scientific success, Pauli's personal life was troubled by his mother's suicide, a bitter divorce and a drinking problem. He sought help from Swiss psychoanalyst Carl Jung, who shared his own mystical views with Pauli throughout many years of correspondence. Pauli once wrote, "I still regard the conceptual aim of overcoming the contrasts, an aim which includes a synthesis embracing the rational understanding as well as the mystic experience of oneness, as the expressed or unspoken mythos of our own present age."

Erwin Schrödinger, an Austrian who was originally more interested in a career as a philosopher than a physicist, developed a different formulation of quantum theory around the same time as Heisenberg. His wave equation described electrons not as individual, localized particles of matter orbiting an atom's nucleus like planets around the sun but rather as standing waves of probability — mere ghosts of particles in the classical sense. Only when such a particle is observed can it be said that it exists in a particular position; unobserved, its position has no existence, only a potentiality for existence.

As Einstein, Bohr and their colleagues were doing their most revolutionary work in continental Europe, British scientists were making their own important contributions. Foremost among them was Sir Arthur Eddington, director of the Cambridge Observatory. Mounting an expedition to Africa to photograph a total solar eclipse in 1919, he produced the first confirmation of Einstein's theory that gravity bends light. A Quaker by upbringing, Eddington was intrigued with the philosophical implications of relativity and quantum theory and authored several books on the subject. In one, Eddington observed that "As truly as the mystic, the scientist is following a light; and it is not a false or an inferior light."

Sir James Jeans, one of Eddington's leading British colleagues, also wrote about physics and philosophy. Jeans is remembered for coining the term "new physics" to describe the work of Bohr, Heisenberg, Schrödinger and others. He did not include Einstein among the "new physicists" but saw him at the end of the "mechanical age" that had started with Sir Isaac Newton.

The Younger Generation

The younger generation of physicists, such as Heisenberg and Pauli, were raised between the World Wars, and faced the moral dilemma of applying physics to inventing weapons of mass destruction.

Robert Oppenheimer, a leading American physicist educated in Europe, was appointed by President Franklin Delano Roosevelt to serve as director of the Manhattan Project, the effort to build the first atomic bomb, at a top-secret installation in Los Alamos, New Mexico. After the war he chaired the Atomic Energy Commission Advisory Committee, where he opposed building larger, more powerful hydrogen bombs — a politically unpopular stance in the early years of the Cold War. In 1953 he was accused of having been a communist sympathizer. Although cleared of treason charges, his security clearance was taken away, along with his government position. He spent his later years as director of Princeton's prestigious Institute for Advanced Study where Einstein had worked for 20 years. Looking back on his distinguished career in physics and its relation to the world, Oppenheimer mused, "The general notions about human understanding illustrated by discoveries in atomic physics are not in the nature of things totally unfamiliar, wholly unheard of, nor new. Even in our own culture they have a history, and in Buddhist and Hindu thought a more considerable and central place. What we shall find is an exemplification, an encouragement, and a refinement of old wisdom."

At age 24, Richard Feynman, one of the most brilliant and eccentric of American physicists, was sent to work on the Manhattan Project. After the war, he made important contributions to modern physics and won the Nobel Prize for his work. He is also celebrated as one of the best teachers of physics, and is remembered for leading the investigation of the Challenger space shuttle disaster. His books included the bestsellers, *Surely You're Joking, Mr. Feynman* and *What Do You Care What Other People Think?*

David Bohm, perhaps the most unusual of the mid-century physicists, worked with the foundations of physics and quantum theory, and authored a respected textbook on quantum theory. Forced to leave the United States during the McCarthy era of the 1950s because he refused as a matter of principle to testify in the congressional hearings against his colleagues such as Oppenheimer, he became an expatriate in Great Britain. In the 1970s,

Bohm initiated a long collaboration and dialogue with the Indian mystic Krishnamurti, and later became a friend of the 14th Dalai Lama, who referred to Bohm as "my physics teacher."

New Physics and Ancient Wisdom

In the last decades of the 20th century, some physicists began writing explicitly about Eastern mysticism as a key to reconciling the paradoxes of the New Physics, and in so doing, pointed the way to the next step in the evolution of human consciousness. First and foremost among them, Fritjof Capra earned his doctorate in particle physics from the University of Vienna in 1966 but soon turned his rational mind toward the challenge of comprehending an initially mystical experience, which he describes in the preface to his now-classic 1976 book, *The Tao of Physics: An Exploration of the Parallels between Modern Physics and Eastern Mysticism*. Sitting by the ocean one afternoon, watching the waves wash against the shore, the California-based physicist realized that the vibrating molecules and atoms composing the scene around him were part of a cosmic dance of energy. "I felt its rhythm and I 'heard' its sound," he recalls, "and at that moment I knew that this was the Dance of Shiva, the Lord of Dancers worshipped by the Hindus."

Other writers soon followed Capra's intellectual-spiritual lead with more books exploring the parallels between the new physics and ancient mysticism. In 1986, philosopher Renee Weber wrote *Dialogues with Scientists and Sages*, in which she presented her conversations with such diverse thinkers as the Dalai Lama, J. Krishnamurti, David Bohm, and Stephen Hawking. In 1995, Victor Mansfield, professor of physics and astronomy at Colgate University merged his scientific research with his studies in Tibetan Buddhism and Jungian psychology in *Synchronicity, Science and Soul-Making*. Amit Goswami, professor of physics at the University of Oregon, described how Eastern mysticism resolves the paradoxes of quantum theory in his book *The Self-Aware Universe*.

Another author who has given voice to the connection between physics and spirituality is Gary Zukav, a non-scientist
who describes himself as a "Harvard grad, Vietnam vet, Green
Beret, recovering soul, and favorite Oprah guest." His book *The
Dancing Wu Li Masters* (1984) stands as a classic in the field.
In his foreword to a later work, *The Seat of the Soul*, Zukav
describes how Niels Bohr and Albert Einstein "saw more than
they could express through the language of...physics, and they
sought to share what they saw. ... They were mystics."

XV

A Glimpse of David Bohm
by Huston Smith

At one point during my decade at Syracuse University the administration entered a line item in its budget to enable the humanities division to bring to the campus each year for three weeks a distinguished visiting professor of humanities. I was appointed to chair the search committee, which consisted of one member from each of the division's five departments.

Saul Bellow for the English Department was an easy choice, as was Noam Chomsky for the philosophers. Next it was the religion department's turn, and (as its representative) I put forward the name of David Bohm. Pandemonium! "You know that the administration gave us this sop to salve its conscience for shortchanging the humanities, and you propose that we give the plum to a *scientist!*" they protested. When the hubbub died down to the point where I could be heard, I admitted that I was indeed doing that, but that I had my reasons. Bohm's doctrine of the implicate order that transcends space and time housed more important implications for religion than anything any religious studies professor we could think of was saying. The committee was not mollified, but I had voted for their candidates, so they had no choice but to vote for mine.

Academic protocol requires that if you officially invite to your campus someone in another field, you clear the invitation with the department in question, so before we invited Bohm I went to the chairman of our physics department to secure his approval. He was ecstatic at the prospect. "Everyone in our department cut his quantum mechanics teeth on Bohm's textbook," he said, and they would all be overjoyed to have him on campus. Could they have him for one of their departmental colloquia? As I was leaving his office, the chairman followed me into the hall to assure me that if I needed more money, just to let him know.

Bohm accepted our invitation, and in due time he arrived for his visit. His three-week stay opened with a Monday evening lecture for the general public. The physics department was out in force.

The physics colloquium took place two days later. When Bohm and I arrived at the departmental office, the chairman welcomed him and then turned him over to several senior professors in order to draw me into the hall. "Huston," he said, "I want to let you know that he will not have a friendly audience." Things Bohm had said in his Monday address had not sat well with the physicists.

When it was time to proceed to the colloquium, we found our way blocked by mobs of faculty and students in the corridors. A backup was in place, and word was circulated that we would proceed to room such-and-such. It too proved inadequate, and what was to have been a colloquium ended as a lecture in the largest hall in the physics building. Even so, some students had to stand throughout the event.

Once introduced, David Bohm mounted the large stage and (without glancing at a note the entire time) talked nonstop for an hour and a quarter as he paced back and forth, covering the three-section, three-tier blackboard with incomprehensible equations. Glancing around the hall, I suspected that within ten minutes he had lost everyone but a handful of senior professors, but he kept on talking. And the audience kept on listening, if for no other reason than to remember for the rest of their lives the experience of watching the workings of the mind of the man who had worked closely with Einstein and whose Hidden-Variable Theory continued to hold out a (minority) hope that Einstein was right in thinking that God does not play dice.

When finally, as abruptly as he had begun, Bohm stopped talking and sat down, the chairman called for questions. Instantly the arm of a senior professor in the front row shot up. "Professor Bohm," the questioner said, "this is all very interesting philosophy. But what does it have to do with physics?" I glanced at the solid bank of equations that stared out at us from the blackboards, with not a single *word* in sight. Without batting an eye, Bohm replied, "I do not make that distinction."

A pall fell over the hall. One or two polite questions brought the afternoon to a close.

I said that I was including this recollection on David Bohm in part to redeem his seeming naivete in defining science so broadly as to include me, and his retort to his questioner does that; for if you do not separate science from philosophy, it does indeed follow that science is unbounded. Whether ultimately the two *can* be separated is too large a question to be entered into here, so I go back now to pick up the question I had begun before David Bohm diverted me. How can science best be defined for purposes of public discourse today?

XVI

Information is Not Transformation

by Larry Dossey

Sensing that something is awry in the way physicians are trained, a common response of medical schools has been to provide students with more information, or with information with a slightly different focus — courses (often optional) in medical ethics, medical humanities, or medical history. But this strategy often makes no real difference, because information is being confused with transformation. The young protohealers are not hungry for more facts but for experiences that can help them connect with those deep psychological and spiritual urges that have manifested throughout history as a commitment to the healing arts.

The informational approach to solving problems in medical education is immensely seductive. It can also be deadly as Neil Postman, chair of the Department of Culture and Communications at New York University, puts it, we have created,

> a new problem never experienced before: information glut, information incoherence, information meaninglessness. ... We have transformed information into a form of garbage, and ourselves into garbage collectors. Like the sorcerer's apprentice, we are awash in information without even a broom to help us get rid of it. Information comes ... at high speeds, severed from import and meaning. And there is no loom to weave it all into fabric. No transcendent narratives to provide us with moral guidance, social purpose, intellectual

economy. No stories to tell us what we need to know, and what we do not need to know.

If our medical schools are once again to produce healers, they will have to foster transformation of the inner life of the students who entrust themselves to the educational process. Postman suggests: "We will need to consult our poets, playwrights, artists, humorists, theologians, and philosophers, who alone are capable of creating or restoring those metaphors and stories that give point to our labors, give meaning to our history, elucidate the present, and give direction to our future."

"Transformation" is a robust project, and we should not underestimate the magnitude of this task. "We're asking a young physician to become a wise old person, and to do it in 4 years of medical school. That's a lot," observed the late molecular biologist and cancer researcher Helene Smith, who believed an infusion of shamanic knowledge into modern medicine would be a good thing. But becoming a wise healer has always been a difficult and lengthy undertaking, even for the shamans. In fact, it was by no means certain that the shaman would survive; the process of transformation sometimes ended in death.

I do not mean to suggest that our medical schools fail completely in their mission. Authentic healers do emerge from them, though not as commonly as they should, and often in spite of the educational process and not because of it. Neither do I wish to imply that the inadequacies we have been addressing are the sole fault of the schools themselves. Medical schools reflect the values of the society in which they exist. If something is amiss in them, the problem can usually be identified in the society as a whole as well. At the root of the problem lies the fact that we, as a culture, have turned our collective back on healing. We should not kid ourselves: we are all in this together, jointly entranced by a physicalistic approach to health and illness and dazzled by the promises of technology to right every conceivable misfire of the body. Against this backdrop, healers and healing have been shoved aside and very nearly forgotten, and we are paying the price. Ignoring the role of consciousness, soul, spirit, and meaning — stock items in the arsenal of authentic healers — we have birthed a malaise that permeates not just the healing profession but our entire society. The casualties have been not just healers and healing but the soul and spirit of a culture.

XVII

Science and the Humanities
by S. Radhakrishnan

[Dr. S. Radhakrishnan (1888-1975) was one of those few great men of this century who distinguished themselves equally in the fields of knowledge as well as that of statesmanship. The following article is taken from his book *True Knowledge*.]

People nowadays are greatly attracted by technological education and naturally, too. But we should also remember that technological education, without the complement of humanistic studies, would be imperfect, lopsided, and deficient. It is possible for us, by the control we have obtained over the forces of nature, to bring about paradise on earth. It is equally possible for us, by pressing a button, to destroy continents. If the choice is to be made wisely, we must be cultivated in the arts of civilized life. Humanistic training and technological study must be regarded as complementary to each other. They should not be regarded as divorced or as separated from each other. ...

Humanities are important because they tell us about our own nature; how we have to grow from day to day. What the impulses are, what the ideals and aspirations are, these are the things that we have to learn from the humanities. But whether it is sciences or humanities, whether they are natural sciences or social sciences, they touch only the periphery of the reality; they touch only the outside, the expression, the multiplicity of manifestations. But what the central being is, you have to learn also if a student is to consider himself to be really educated.

Mere sciences, natural or social, are not enough. You have to exercise yourself, what is called some kind of solitary reflection or if we wish to follow up political revolution by a social and economic one, our universities must send out batches of scientists, technicians, engineers, agriculturists, and so forth. These are essential for changing the face of our country, the economic character of our society. But we should not believe that science and technology alone are enough. There are other countries, much advanced countries in the world, which have achieved marvelous progress in scientific and technological areas, but yet they are torn by strife and are unable to bring about peace, safety, and security of their own people. It only shows that other qualities are also necessary besides those developed by science and technology.

The function of the universities is not merely to send out technically skilled and professionally competent men, but it is their duty to produce in them the quality of compassion, the quality, which enables the individuals to treat one another in a truly democratic spirit. Our religions have proclaimed from the very beginning, that each human individual is to be regarded as a spark of the Divine. That Thou Art, *Tat tvam asi,* is the teaching of the Upanishads.

That is why even though our country needs great scientists, great technologists, great engineers, we should not neglect to make them humanists. While we retain science and technology we must remember that science and technology are not all. We must note the famous statement that merely by becoming literate without the development of compassion we become demoniac. So no university can regard itself as a true university unless it sends out young men and women who are not only learned but whose hearts are full of compassion for the suffering humanity. Unless that is there, the university education must be regarded as incomplete.

No one can be said to be truly educated if his knowledge is limited to one special branch. The evils of specialization can be combated only by a course in what is now called general education.

National education does not mean that subjects like physics and chemistry, engineering and technology, change with the boundaries of nations. It means that there is a national heritage, a tradition of values into which the students should be initiated. India is not a geographical abstraction but a living spirit. The outlook associated with the country has been a spiritual one, that there are higher laws of the universe than those studied by sciences and technology, that the world is more than what we see, feel, touch, and measure. Two principle features of the modern world are that *we are members one of another,* that there is no decree of God or man which compels us to be sick and hungry, poor and unemployed. The strong shall help the weak is the foundation of all civilized existence.

It is also possible to unify the world and all of us can settle down as good neighbors. A future more glorious than the past is open to us. And yet we are afraid of what lies before us, for we see that there is no limit to the possibilities of scientific destruction. The obstacles to human well-being are in the minds of men. Hatred, folly, erroneous beliefs and uncivil passions make us incapable of seeing the truth and working for it. To counter these tendencies we need, in addition to technological knowledge and skill, an understanding heart, and wisdom. It is because of the lack of wisdom that many of us are mentally unstable and morally unsound.

Wisdom and Knowledge

As the *Bhagavad Gītā* has it, we should aim at wisdom as well as knowledge, *jñānam vijñāna sahitam.* At a time when we are obsessed with technical achievement rather than with absolute values, with practical work rather than with a full life, it is good to realize that technology is for man and not man for technology. The material things of the world are to be used for expanding man's knowledge and enriching the treasures of the spirit. It is not enough to feed the human animal or train the human mind. We must also attend to the needs of the human spirit. We must learn to live from a new basis, discover the reserves of spirituality, the sense of the sacred found in all religions.

The aim of the natural scientist is to discover the external world of reality. By scientific methods we do not know anything directly about reality. Scientific information is indefinite and uncertain in its import. It gives us signs, which we have to interpret. The scientist assumes that the world is governed by a system of laws, which can be understood, though not in a comprehensive way. The only interpretation that is logical is that which points to a central mystery. We know only in part, not the beginning, not the end. We should admit that the mystery is not capable of adequate logical description or linguistic statement. We should not only be tolerant, but appreciative of others' points.

There is, however, no incompatibility between the findings of science and the doctrines of religion. The search of truth is their common goal though they have different ways of approach to it. Since God is Truth, *satya-svarūpa,* the quest of Truth is the quest of God. Man who makes the machine is greater than the machine. He who splits the atom is greater than the atom. Science does not suggest the omnipotence of matter. It suggests the supremacy of the spirit of man. The spirit, which moves in the minds of the men and inspires and guides them in this quest, is divine. The word *Brahman* connotes both the truth, which is sought, and the spirit in us, which seeks it. A scientific view of the world reveals to us a central mystery that is not disclosed to scientific observation. Our attitude to it should be one of piety, humility, and adoration. We must acknowledge that truth belongs to God and ideas belong to men. The poison of intolerance is inconsistent with the mystery of God. Too much blood has been unnecessarily and unjustly shed in the name of religious doctrine. The different religions are great spiritual achievements of man and we should take pride not in one special production of mankind but in all, for all are fellow pilgrims treading our way to the truth in every great faith. *Tirukkural* is claimed by the followers of Jainism, Buddhism, and Hinduism, and teaches a universal humanism. True religion requires us to extend our sympathy even to those who do not belong to our group. Religious pride may make us hold that true religion is our own, that "we are the people, and wisdom shall die with us."

Religion Rightly Interpreted

Science enlarges our concepts of God, and religion saves science from going astray. Religion should not end in wars and inquisitions, or science in Hiroshimas and Nagasakis. It is said that a man without religion is like a horse without a bridle. We need the discipline of religion to civilize our nature, to restrain the greed, the callousness, and the brutality in us. Religion, however, should not be interpreted in a narrow, sectarian, dogmatic sense; but in the broad sense indicated by our great seers and *bhakta,* the *nayanars,* the *alvars,* and the *ācārya.* They are united in telling us that we will not be able to create an ordered society unless we learn to master ourselves. In the disordered and bewildered world in which we live, we must learn to live by the values the religious thinkers set before us. We can have peace only if we have the courage of renunciation. Through illness, poverty, or death, we begin to feel that the world is not made for us. However beautiful our dreams may be, circumstances may forbid them. In such situations courage is what we need most. Our country has been passing through a series of very rapid changes in recent times. We have had religious reforms initiated in our times by Ram Mohan Roy, Ramakrishna, Vivekananda, Tagore, and others. We have had social reform movements started also by the same agencies. Gandhi gave us the political revolution. He asked us to shed off the shame of subjection, become independent and stand erect on our feet and not always walk on our knees. ...

This country, during its great days, was never isolated. It was a part of the stream of world history. If you turn to the ancient systems of mathematics or medicine, and so forth, you will find there the great influence of the Greek, the Roman, the West Asian, and other systems. If you turn to the European world you will find that the great advances of science were due to the cooperation of people like Newton, an Englishman; Kepler, a German; Copernicus, a Pole; Galileo, an Italian. All of them collaborated and brought about a scientific revolution of the modern world. So also we were collaborating with the other nations in our great days. When we fell under subjection, when we were cut off from the other sources, when we became isolated, our lives became constricted, and we were not able to carry the torch that we used to. After political independence was gained, we again came back into the mainstream of history. Our scientists go to different parts of the world and make some small contributions to the advance of the world. They are known today to all parts of the world where science is pursued and, therefore, it is a matter of great significance, that we have come back: and that the gospel that we adopted and which we practiced for a number of years we forgot it, we were cut off from it, and we have come back to it, and, therefore, we must try to regain our lost initiative.

Adopt a Scientific Outlook

It is necessary that if we want to attack the problems which our country faces — poverty, malnutrition, disease, defective water supply, people dying like flies in some parts of the country — these are all things which must make us feel ashamed of ourselves — it is necessary for us to care for the poor. Attention to the poor is the supreme test by which any government is judged. If we are to be judged to be a civilized society, our first interest must be what we are doing for the thousands of people who are suffering from undreamt of evils — who are the victims, so to say, of all sorts of epidemics and we died like flies on the pavements of our country or in rural areas. If we want to tackle these problems it is essential for us to develop science and technology. We must develop these things; we must adopt a scientific outlook. Everyone of us must be endowed with a scientific spirit; obscurantism, superstition, and such other things that have weighed us down for centuries must be removed and human beings must feel that they are rational human beings with dignity, with a sense of responsibility, responsibility not merely for what they do but for the poor who are entrusted to their care.

Again and again remarks were made, a special lecture was delivered at Cambridge, saying that a scientific culture and an academic or literary culture are two different things and one has little to do with the other. We produce either seers or technicians; we produce men of intuition, of imagination, or we produce men with mechanical skill with practical ability, but we do not produce men who are at the same time seers and technicians, people who are able to develop their imagination and at the same time develop their scientific skill. This whole concept of our cultures being divided, of their being two, is something that is, to my mind, unfounded. Truth is indivisible. Whether it is historic truth, literary truth, or scientific truth, the approaches may be different, but ultimately what we do is exactly the same. It is the imagination that is roused in us by the study of literature, it is imagination again that makes the scientist go forward; his hypothesis makes him remold the environment by which he is presented and makes him bring out the deepest secrets of nature. It is the spirit in man that sits in judgment on the facts of nature, which enables the human being to reshape the environment. We should reshape not merely our outer environment but our inner environment also, our inward forces, the internal power we have, even that has to be remolded.

The great leaders of countries, the great statesmen, have developed astounding power over nature; they have developed spectacular capacity to destroy humanity as well as to save humanity. If we are threatened today by the forces that we have raised, it is not due to forces outside, but to lack of control which we have, so to say. It is not weapons that destroy us but it is lack of wisdom. It is the human being who destroys the rest of humanity. If we are to reform ourselves, then science will be the great instrument for the development of the human race, for improving the quality of the human race. That is what we should aim at. *Ātma Saṁskṛti*: development of human nature, refinement of the human spirit — that is the one supreme aim, which we have to put before ourselves.

S. RADHAKRISHNAN

Study Science in Depth

Most of us think that we are scientists because we press a button, the light comes up; we press another button, the telephone rings; we press a third button, we get the car outside. But we do not know how these things function. What is the knowledge that is enshrined in these instruments? We know only how to press a button and get something done. That is, we live on the surface of human life — robots, mechanics, technicians. We do not know what the depths of these things indicate and stand for. If we know that, we will never say that science is a different discipline and not a human discipline, and the other things, literature, history, and so forth, make a different kind of man. It is not so. We must study science, not from the surface, but from its very depth. We must try to understand how all these things happen, how the human being has been able to penetrate into these things, and how it has brought about a new transformed world. It is not necessary for us to be technologically or mechanically uniform. That does not follow. If we have the human spirit cultivated, we will not become mere mechanical robots. The very transformation that science has brought about will make you raise the question of the meaning of existence. That is part of the quest for knowledge. You want to know why knowledge is what it is, what is the knowledge which science contributes, what is the relation to the knowledge which other branches of discipline give us.

All the branches of discipline have only one end — *sarvaśāstra prayojanam ātma darśanam.* An insight into Reality is the end of all kinds of discipline. You must recognize that knowledge cannot be divided against itself. All truth must be regarded as one whole. Whether you practice this discipline or the other discipline, you should practice the one supreme pursuit of truth. It is that which makes a human being dignified and civilized. If you are able to do it, then you become a really civilized human being.

There is a general criticism leveled against us that, where our knowledge of nature is increasing, our wisdom is diminishing. The achievements of science are spectacular, and they have obtained such great power in their control that they can devastate the world. If there are people who contemplate the results of nuclear developments, they will feel what is it that has happened to man, why is it that he has increased in worldly power, has so much extended his body through his control over radio, television, and other machines, and yet his soul seems to be stagnant? It is not growing correspondingly. There is disproportion between the growth of wisdom and the increase of knowledge. It is that disparity that has impressed many people. Let us try to extend our understanding of the nature of things; let us have certain values that will be utilized by the mechanical devices and contrivances we have brought about. It is necessary for us to know, whatever may be the nature of science, it is the spirit of man that is expressing itself there. Every human individual must look up to himself, not as living on the outer surface of things. There is a living depth in him. There is a center there that persists, that abides, whatever may be the changes. Vacaspati tells us: "That which abides in the revolving world, in the rotating wheel of time, where all things are revolving, there is still a center." If we merely live on the surface of things, if we are dealing with machines and make ourselves into machines, this danger will become really great and we will get alienated from our true spirit. So it is that whatever be our knowledge, scientific or humanistic, understand it as the expression of the wondrous mind of man, beautiful spirit, which is there, the liquid flame of consciousness. If we look at the surface of things, we overlook the reality that is the supreme source of everything great. We have to see if this side of knowledge is increasing, if wisdom is diminishing.

If that kind of criticism is hurled against us, it is due to neglect of the spiritual side, due to the neglect of human beings who are concentrating themselves on the externals of life, little realizing that these externals are to be employed for the purpose of promoting human wisdom. So wisdom and knowledge will have to grow together. Everything in this world has been a means or an instrument of grasping of the Eternal. Even the arts in which we dwell, the arts that we foster, they are said to be — "That by which we grasp the Eternal, that is said to be an art," and its purpose is to refine the spirit of man. All sciences are there, but we are incapable of using them for refining our own spirit. We have said it so often but in our practice we overlook it.

There is some spiritual inadequacy, bordering on illiteracy, among the graduates of our country. They go through their routine, they pass their examinations, and yet do not seem to know what the first principles of Indian culture are!

If we live today, it is not because of our great industrial progress or mechanical efficiency or our atom bombs and things like that. We live today because there are still people who illustrate for the commonalty the path of spirituality and their behavior is something, which is divinely ordained. It is such people who represent the true culture of our country, *adhyātma vidyā*; of all sciences, the greatest science is the knowledge of your own Self.

XVIII

Science and Ethics
by Amit Goswami

Ethical actions are those taken with consideration and compassion for others. The Golden Rule of ethics appears in all religions. For example:

- HINDUISM: This is the sum of duty; do naught unto others, which if done to thee will cause thee pain.
- ZOROASTRIANISM: That nature alone is good which refrains from doing unto another whatsoever is not good for itself:
- TAOISM: Regard your neighbor's gain as your own gain, and your neighbor's loss as your own loss.
- BUDDHISM: Hurt not others in ways you would find hurtful.
- CONFUCIANISM: Do not unto others what you would not have them do unto you.
- JAINISM: In happiness and suffering, in joy and grief, we should regard all creatures as we regard our own self.
- JUDAISM: Whatever you hatest thyself, that do not do to another.
- CHRISTIANITY: All things whatsoever ye would that men should do to you, do ye ever so to them.
- ISLAM: No one of you is a believer until he desires for his brother that which he desires for himself.
- SIKHISM: As thou deemest thyself, so deem others. (Iyer 1983, 36)

In the light of materialist science, the question of ethics is puzzling. The only basic value that materialists can come up with is the necessity of survival. Genes want to perpetuate themselves. Acting altruistically may be beneficial to a "gene machine" (such as ourselves), because to the extent that we share genes with the person we help, we are also helping our own genes to survive and propagate. In this view, our ethical responsibility moves concentrically — from our parents or children to our siblings, then to cousins, then to people of our own clan with whom we intermarry, and so forth. But the study of altruistic people does not agree with this narrow view (Ray 1996).

If biology cannot settle the issue, can philosophy? There are two notable philosophies of ethics: the philosophy of utilitarianism, developed by Bentham and Mill, and the philosophy of Immanuel Kant. Utilitarianism is particularly consonant with the spirit of materialism; ethics becomes a convenience to ensure the greatest good for the greatest number. Speaking as a proponent of idealism, Kant suggested that we follow the ways of ethics, because of a categorical imperative, conscience. Is there any scientific basis for this categorical imperative? What does idealist science have to say about this?

If consciousness collapses quantum possibility into actuality and we are that consciousness, then certainly it would seem that we choose and are responsible for our actions. Alas, it is not that simple. To the extent that we are identified with our ego, we do not exercise freedom of choice. Our actions are reactive, defensive, and conditioned. We are unable to choose and, therefore, unable to bear responsibility.

Given that most people's identities are defined by and limited to the conditioned ego, the materialist ethic of the greatest good for the greatest number serves to protect the innocent from conditioned criminal behavior. True idealist ethics holds only when we begin to feel conscience or a Kantian imperative to follow ethics. Then the Golden Rule makes complete sense: I will not hurt another because the other is me. When we undertake the spiritual journey beyond ego, ethics becomes an important tool, a creative path to follow on our way (Goswami 1993).

Ethics and Love

What is the role of ethical action in spiritual practice? Why should consideration and compassion for others help us shift beyond the ego's bondage and limitation?

Selfish or unethical actions, which are conditioned, invariably produce the doubt: Am I doing the right thing? The voice of conscience (*viveka* in Sanskrit) tears us apart. The more conflict there is between our actions and our conscience, the more constricted our consciousness becomes. Compassionate action, on the other hand, expands our consciousness and immediately produces the happiness that comes with expansion.

Moreover, since the ego operates in a simple hierarchy, when we are identified with our ego we look at the world hierarchically, with ourselves at the top of the hierarchy. All causal narrative begins with me; all causal importance is attributed to me. I can love you but only if you are "mine" in some way: my spouse, my child, my lover or friend, my countryman. The ego's world is solipsistic; only "I" am real, all else is my extension.

In contrast, the quantum self is tangled-hierarchical in relationship with the objects of its awareness. The subject and object are split but co-dependent. There is experience but no personal self that experiences. There is only the verb — the subject and the object are implicit.

Our action is truly ethical when it is moved spontaneously by unconditional love and compassion, when only the verb — only loving, free of hierarchy — defines the action. Acting from this place, we fall into the tangled hierarchy of the quantum self, abandoning the simple hierarchy of the limited ego. So ethical action, like ritual, is a vehicle for spiritual growth.

From another standpoint, seldom is an act good or evil in itself; its moral value depends on the context, which is often somewhat ambiguous. For this reason, ethics is not a matter of following a moral rule absolutely in all circumstances. That is fanaticism. Moral decisions confront us with choice and responsibility in a way that demands a creative response. If we enter the creative process, when we take the quantum leap, the ethical choice arises spontaneously from insight, not from deliberation, which is limited and often self-serving.

Our internal state is more difficult to look at than we acknowledge; it is much easier to preach to others. For instance, the path of peace activism seems easy at the outset, but it is often betrayed because of the activist's own inner violence. The American mystic, known as Peace Pilgrim, suffered many ups and downs before peace became truly stabilized in her actions (Peace Pilgrim, 1982).

In terms of the Hindu concept of *yugas*, there is a reason for emphasizing unselfish altruism in these times. Three *yugas* (eras) have preceded the current one, the *Kali-yuga*. In the earlier *yugas* we were much less identified with our egos, the distractions were less compelling, the separateness less intense, and the return journey to unity less arduous. Who now has the time for a rigorous practice of meditation, Patanjali-style? This is why the wise say: In the *Kali-yuga*, go directly for God's grace. Love someone unconditionally, serve somebody, and remember God. "My religion is kindness," says the Dalai Lama. Make loving kindness your religion. In the *kali-yuga*, that is enough.

We seem to know this intuitively. With the present materialism and distracting technology in the West, we may think that altruism should be at an all-time low. But a recent survey shows that it is on an upswing. More than twenty percent of Americans engage in altruism (Ray, 1996).

The Reincarnational Context

Unlike physical laws, ethical laws are not inviolable. However, this does not entitle us to live unethically, even if we are not spiritually inclined. According to the law of *karma*, every action done intentionally has both immediate and long-term effects. In the context of the scheme of reincarnation, this means that loving another moves us toward spiritually, while harming another sets up karmic reverberations that may take lifetimes to resolve. Understood in these terms, we are wise to avoid the negative results of harming another. Otherwise, we pay for it in another life.

Why do bad things happen to good people? Religions without a reincarnational doctrine constantly struggle with this question. One answer is to simply acknowledge the role of conditioned forces acting on the multiple parts of a complex system. But one can, with some legitimacy, counter that such conditioning is itself part of God's design. And so the question remains.

According to the theories of reincarnation and *karma*, bad things that happen to people who are ethical and creative provide opportunities to recover from negative propensities acquired in past lives; that is, they are opportunities to burn up past *karma*. The arrows released in ignorance from your bow must fly their course, for good or ill. It is God's design that the conditioning not only of this life, but of past lives influences our actions. The universe is a school, of sorts; we learn to know ourselves in order to gain our most creative destiny. To learn is to take responsibility for our mistakes, and then to correct our mistakes, even those accrued in past lives.

XIX

Deepening Our Purpose
John Templeton and Rebekah Dunlap

Are we at a time in human evolution where it could be helpful for humanity if more research was directed toward understanding some of the basic spiritual realities such as prayer, love, worship, thanksgiving, and humility? How might individuals benefit from this knowledge? Could researching these realities offer a source of creative possibilities that might flourish, were we to consider humbly our role in the quest to discover more of sublime purposes? How could this research help us learn more about why we are created? What areas of daily living could be enhanced from this type of research?

If we approach life in humility of spirit, with an attitude of loving service, how could our purposes make a difference in our world? Have we considered that helping others to discover their purpose might be part of our purpose? Are there various levels of purpose and sometimes changes in direction of purpose? Purpose can range in scope from a primal fight for survival to the highest level of intellectual and spiritual aspiration and expression. Purpose can also change with regard to the circumstances of life. Is it then worth the effort to explore and attempt to discover ongoing purpose throughout our lives? Should we be enthusiastically interested in welcoming and exploring the most simple or the most complex ideas? Could these ideas help us enlarge our personal and global spiritual vision, better comprehend how tiny and temporary we are and how much we have yet to discover?

What inspirational challenges might enrich our understanding with concepts and perspectives that may lead to new discoveries and creative improvements? Can devout participation in a religious or spiritual life sometimes serve as a strong motivator and inspiration in the formation of beneficial qualities of good character? How can the act of worship serve as an invitation to discover higher spiritual energies? How can worship assist us in learning various lessons of life? Is every thought, feeling, and action actually some kind of prayer? What newly discovered wisdom might be found in researching inspired thoughts from the great thinkers and writers from various cultures and religious perspectives?

The Blessings of Personal Spiritual Values

Do we experience a shift of personal values when we lift our vision from worldly accomplishment to spiritual discoveries? If so, how does this shift in focus help propel us toward beneficial accomplishments? What do you think are basic spiritual realities? How high would attributes of praise, gratitude, noble purpose, humility, and thanksgiving, for example, rate on your list of character traits and beneficial qualities? How could trust and openness, sensitivity, creativity, stability, honesty, integrity, worship, and devotion help us discover divine purposes? Could we then direct our actions for the greater good of humanity?

Many people cherish dreams and goals aligned with their personal desires. However, when we lift our vision to Spirit's guidance, do we feel expanded and more deeply connected to higher purposes? Certainly, our lives often seem to take on deeper meaning as we invite the energies of unlimited love, compassion, and radiant spiritual light to be guiding forces in our daily activities. Dr. Viktor Frankl affirms Nietzsche's words, "He who has a why to live for can bear with almost any how." The point is that purpose and meaning can be experienced in many aspects of life.

What steps can we take to explore avenues for creative purpose? What are we willing to do in the present moment?

Is a clear process available that could help build a bridge of greater understanding between the visible and invisible realms, the physical and spiritual planes?

Food for Body, Mind, and Spirit

Would you think of going without eating regular meals for a week? For two weeks? For three weeks? Probably not! The human body needs life-nourishing food on a regular basis to remain healthy. Without the various nutrients provided by food, the vital energy to keep our muscles firm and strong and our ability to stay active could deteriorate. Our mental processes would slow. Without food, symptoms of malnutrition might soon become evident and we would likely lose the ability to function effectively. Would we foolishly ignore our symptoms, or would we take immediate steps to remedy the situation?

Every living organism needs food for sustenance. Even simple vegetable cells need nourishment. Guided by innate intelligence, the plant absorbs the food that is essential to its growth and development. When grown in a soil and climate that is conducive to growth, the plant flourishes. If grown in soil and climate conditions that are impoverished and devitalized, a corresponding degenerative plant specimen may result.

As we need food on a regular basis to sustain our body's energy, is it not also logical that our soul needs nourishment on a regular basis to maintain spiritual health? What happens when we go without regular spiritual nourishment? (And a quick, occasional "snack" does not get the job done!) We could become mentally, physically, and emotionally unstable. We may feel fearful, or inadequate or depleted. We may feel isolated and alone. We might lose our optimistic attitude and become easily upset, angry, or judgmental. We may become sharp and abrasive to others. Relationships may crumble. Our personalities may lose their sparkle. And what happens to our feelings of unlimited love, noble purpose, and high vision? Without spiritual nourishment, are we more likely to become sidetracked from our purposes? Many religions and spiritual traditions refer to a vibratory energy at the core of our being as the divine spark, a higher power, the Spirit, the soul essence, the seat of the sacred, or Spirit's essence. How important is it to reconnect on a regular basis with the inner Spirit to build up reserves of love, wisdom, and self-mastery that far surpass our human resources?

Divine energy is a boundless source of spiritual sustenance, eternally ready and infinitely available. We may feast from the table of spiritual bounty at any time. And what could be more "delicious" and soul satisfying than the spiritual qualities that multiply our blessings, help us discover our purpose in life, and lead us to understanding why we are created?

The Benefits of Praise and Thanksgiving

Praise implies an expression of approval, esteem, or commendation. We praise a superb performance. We acknowledge a job well done with sincere words of approval and encouragement. We sing praises to the glory of God. "Praise God from whom all blessings flow!" Praise can help us eliminate stress from our lives by directing our thoughts and mind to be more in tune with the Infinite.

From where do many of the stresses and conflicts in our world arise? Could some of the problems experienced in human life be a result of ignorance? When people seem ignorant of spiritual realities and life purposes, can their values become confused, resulting in inappropriate choices and actions? Could the focus of individual thoughts and feelings be part of the problem? What results might be experienced if, in a stressful situation, conflictive thoughts were halted and replaced with the simple statement: "Praise God for the gift of my life?"

Praising God for life can affirm an attitude of praise and gratitude with the Creator's spirit within. How may resolution of stress, confusion, and inner conflict lead us into increased spiritual growth? How could the words "Praise God for the gift of my life" urge us to reach for higher values or challenge us to explore new areas of discovery? New possibilities often present themselves in the most amazing ways! We may be astounded when we look beyond appearances and uncover the precious treasure of a person or an experience.

Gratitude and thanksgiving are spiritual tools, similar to praise, for transforming many of the stresses and challenges of modern life. Both gratitude and thanksgiving express grateful acknowledgment and feelings of thankful appreciation for benefits received. These spiritual attributes often open the door to increased growth, because they embrace the purpose of creation within itself. True thanksgiving has been described as the soul's recognition of its relation to the Creator. When this recognition occurs, could there be any limit to the soul's capacity for beneficial and fruitful accomplishment?

PART FOUR

The Sages Speak

*The sages of the Upanishads discovered
the center of the universe in the center of man.
Through that discovery,
man was revealed in his infinite dimension
and the universe was also revealed in its spiritual glory.*

Swami Ranganathananda

Happiness is the goal of both science and religion. The question is how do we achieve that goal? Science would have us achieve happiness based on our senses and intellect through inquiry into the objective world. On the other hand, religious scriptures tell us that the search for happiness is subjective and begins within us, that we need to inquire into our real nature. The quest for happiness arises only in man, for only he has intellect, and the intellect wants to know the truth of what we see, whether through science, religion, or both. The search for Truth can take different paths, and accordingly can yield different results. One path leads to success. The other path leads to failure. Religion says that as long as we use instruments — whether they are our senses, machines, or equipment — we limit ourselves and will fail to discover the Truth.

Even man's mind is a limiting instrument that by itself cannot see the Truth. Science will set goals and objectives, and through its instruments will make discoveries, but will never see the Truth. The Truth can only be seen (or experienced) successfully through man's power of concentration. In religion one can transcend his own limits and see the Truth. No instruments — or medium of any kind — are required. Science is limited in another way; it cannot give us moral direction. We have guided missiles, but misguided minds. When properly understood and applied by people of pure minds, religion and science can bring blessings to the world. All sciences are based on the human intellect. So, why is religion — Vedanta, specifically — called the science of sciences? because it points toward the origin of the intellect. *Brahma vidyā* is the foundation of all.

Swami Tejomayananda

XX

An Appeal
by The Dalai Lama

Within less than fifty years, I, Tenzin Gyatso, the Buddhist monk, will be no more than a memory. Indeed, it is doubtful whether a single person reading these words will be alive a century from now. Time passes unhindered. When we make mistakes, we cannot turn the clock back and try again. All we can do is use the present well. Therefore, if, when our final day comes, we are able to look back and see that we have lived full, productive, and meaningful lives, that will at least be of some comfort. If we cannot, we may be very sad. But which of these we experience is up to us.

The best way to ensure that when we approach death we do so without remorse is to ensure that in the present moment we conduct ourselves responsibly and with compassion for others. Actually, this is in our own interest, and not just because it will benefit us in the future. As we have seen, compassion is one of the principal things that make our lives meaningful. It is the source of all lasting happiness and joy. And it is the foundation of a good heart, the heart of one who acts out of a desire to help others. Through kindness, through affection, through honesty, through truth and justice toward all others we ensure our own benefit. This is not a matter for complicated theorizing. It is a matter of common sense. There is no denying that consideration of others is worthwhile. There is no denying that our happiness is inextricably bound up with the happiness of others. There is no denying that if society suffers, we ourselves suffer. Nor is there any denying that the more our hearts and minds are afflicted with ill will, the more miserable we become. Thus we can reject everything else: religion, ideology, all received wisdom. But we cannot escape the necessity of love and compassion.

This, then, is my true religion, my simple faith. In this sense, there is no need for temple or church, for mosque or synagogue, no need for complicated philosophy, doctrine, or dogma. Our own heart, our own mind, is the temple. The doctrine is compassion. Love for others and respect for their rights and dignity, no matter who or what they are: ultimately these are all we need. So long as we practice these in our daily lives, then no matter if we are learned or unlearned, whether we believe in Buddha or God, or follow some other religion or none at all, as long as we have compassion for others and conduct ourselves with restraint out of a sense of responsibility, there is no doubt we will be happy.

Why, then, if it is so simple to be happy, do we find it so hard? Unfortunately, though most of us think of ourselves as compassionate, we tend to ignore these commonsense truths. We neglect to confront our negative thoughts and emotions. Unlike the farmer who follows the seasons and does not hesitate to cultivate the land when the moment comes, we waste so much of our time in meaningless activity. We feel deep regret over trivial matters like losing money, while keeping from doing what is genuinely important without the slightest feeling of remorse. Instead of rejoicing in the opportunity we have to contribute to others' well-being, we merely take our pleasures where we can. We shrink from considering others on the grounds that we are too busy. We run right and left, making calculations and telephone calls and thinking that this would be better than that. We do one thing but worry that if something else comes along we had better do another. But in this we engage only in the coarsest and most elementary levels of the human spirit. Moreover, by being inattentive to the needs of others, inevitably we end up harming them. We think ourselves very clever, but how do we use our abilities? All too often we use them to deceive our neighbors, to take advantage of them and better ourselves at their expense. And when things do not work out, full of self-righteousness, we blame them for our difficulties.

Yet lasting satisfaction cannot be derived from the acquisition of objects. No matter how many friends we acquire, they cannot make us happy. And indulgence in sensual pleasure is nothing but a gateway to suffering. It is like honey smeared along the cutting edge of a sword. Of course, that is not to say that we should despise our bodies. On the contrary, we cannot be of help to others without a body. But we need to avoid the extremes that can lead to harm.

In focusing on the mundane, what is essential remains hidden from us. Of course, if we could be truly happy doing so, then it would be entirely reasonable to live like this. Yet we cannot. At best, we get through life without too much trouble. But then when problems assail us, as they must, we are unprepared. We find that we cannot cope. We are left despairing and unhappy.

Therefore, with my two hands joined, I appeal to you, the reader, to ensure that you make the rest of your life as meaningful as possible. Do this by engaging in spiritual practice if you can. As I hope I have made clear, there is nothing mysterious about this. It consists in nothing more than acting out of concern for others. And provided you undertake this practice sincerely and with persistence, little by little, step by step you will gradually be able to reorder your habits and attitudes so that you think less about your own narrow concerns and more of others. In doing so, you will find that you enjoy peace and happiness yourself.

Relinquish your envy, let go your desire to triumph over others. Instead, try to benefit them. With kindness, with courage, and with confidence that in doing so you are sure to meet with success, welcome others with a smile. Be straightforward. And try to be impartial. Treat everyone as though they were a close friend. I say this neither as Dalai Lama nor as someone who has special powers or ability. Of these I have none. I speak as a human being: one who, like yourself, wishes to be happy and not to suffer.

If you cannot, for whatever reason, be of help to others, at least don't harm them. Consider yourself a tourist. Think of the world as it is seen from space, so small and insignificant yet so beautiful. Could there really be anything to be gained from harming others during our stay here? Is it not preferable, and more reasonable, to relax and enjoy ourselves quietly, just as if we were visiting a different neighborhood? Therefore, if in the midst of your enjoyment of the world you have a moment, try to help in however small a way those who are downtrodden and those who, for whatever reason, cannot or do not help themselves. Try not to turn away from those whose appearance is disturbing, from the ragged and unwell. Try never to think of them as inferior to yourself. If you can, try not even to think of yourself as better than the humblest beggar. You will look the same in your grave.

To close with, I would like to share a short prayer that gives me great inspiration in my quest to benefit others:

May I become at all times both now and forever
A protector for those without protection
A guide for those who have lost their way
A ship for those with oceans to cross
A bridge for those with rivers to cross
A sanctuary for those in danger
A lamp for those without light
A place of refuge for those who lack shelter
And a servant to all in need.

XXI

Higher Values
Add Value to Life

by Swami Tejomayananda

[From a talk delivered on October 24, 2004 at Sai International Centre, Delhi.]

All around us we see a lot of chaos, commotion, and destruction, and we hear the concerns of many about moral degradation and the loss of human values. We are taught that God is all pervading, but we see that corruption is all pervading. As a result, people are concerned and worried about the future. Such situations are not new. Our scriptures contain descriptions similar to today's prevailing state of affairs. If you read Sage Narada's description of life on this earth, without knowing the context, one would imagine that it is a description of the present times. Socrates deplored the indiscipline and disobedience of the children of those days. So, what is happening today is not new.

When we say that human values are deteriorating, we must be clear about what these human values are, how they are worsening, and what we can do to restore them. People are doing what they can at various levels to address the situation, through seminars, workshops, and conferences. Deep within our hearts each of us knows what to do, but when it comes to action, we compromise.

A journalist once asked me, "Aren't you alarmed by the present condition of the youth?" He was surprised when I replied,

"No, I am not concerned." Human beings have the free will to destroy themselves and conversely, they also have the ability to rebuild what has been devastated. This is the beauty of human nature. There is a familiar saying, "All that goes up, must come down." The flip side is, "All that has come down, must go up." Hence, we should not let the situation depress us; it does not help.

One reason for today's decline into decadence is that we give more importance to things than to values. The second point to consider is that material objects are not the most important things in life. Every person has the inherent desire to enrich his or her life. We want security, followed by more and more comfort, and then greater pleasure. We want a bigger house and more things around us. These are signs of prosperity. Based on this we call a nation "developed." Those that have more material objects, a higher per capita income, and the ability to spend more money are labeled "prosperous."

Outer and Inner Enrichment

Enrichment has two aspects — outer and inner. For the moment, let me focus on the first. To enrich our outer life, we require a lot of effort and money. However, some of the basic — and valuable — necessities of life are free. We can live without gold, silver, and jewels, but not without air, space, solar energy, and water, which are given to us free. While the space we live in is free, we put a price on the land and commercialize it. Tulsidasji, the great poet of the epic, *Rāma Carita Mānasa,* says that God has made the luxuries like precious stones, gold, and silver high in price, but out of compassion for us, He has made all the necessities of life free.

We take all of Mother Nature's gifts for granted. Using the raw materials provided by Her, we turn them into different sizes and shapes and we continue to make things more valuable. We delight in having something that another person does not have and at the same time we don't want to be outdone by our neighbor. When we ascribe value to material objects, we create competition. In the world of cutthroat competition, the principle of "live and let live" is replaced by "kill or get killed." On the other hand, air is something that all of us breathe at the same time and there is no competition. But when we give value to limited, manmade objects, and associate prestige, and power to them, we cause competition and greed.

We call ourselves superior and intelligent beings while continuing to destroy the very ecology, such as plants, trees, and animals, on which our wellbeing depends. The plant and animal kingdom can exist very comfortably without human beings, but we cannot live without them. The task of anyone superior is to protect the inferior. In a family, the role of the protector falls on the older sibling. Those who are more educated must look after those who are less educated. The strong must look after the weak.

None of these values are heeded because there is undue importance being given to money. We blame money, but really money is not to be blamed. Material objects have become more important to us than values. Our outer lives can be made prosperous by all the trappings of wealth and luxury, but what about those values that enrich us inwardly? Without virtues like love, compassion, and honesty, we cannot have a meaningful life.

At a railway station, an obese man stood on a weighing machine, but since it was out of order, the needle did not move. After waiting expectantly for a few moments, he stepped off the scales. Two little boys standing nearby began to whisper to each other. One little boy said to the other, "I told you he was hollow." The man symbolizes the hollowness of the outwardly prosperous. Such people are usually fearful of being cheated of their wealth. They feel that they have something that is coveted by others and hence live in a constant state of insecurity. Such people are indeed to be pitied because they cannot love or trust anyone.

The virtues that beautify our inner life are free. Tulsidasji said, "To chant the name of God requires no money. To speak good and sweet words, nothing extra is required." All human beings, even the birds and plants, are moved by the power of kind words. The words we use can show either our inner enrichment or how impoverished our minds are.

Worship *(pūjā)* is done at two levels — external and internal (mental). At the external level, we may not have the means to offer a golden throne or expensive ornaments to the Lord, but that does not mean that we cannot offer the best mentally. We require a lot of effort, and depend on external means to make our outer life richer, but to enrich our inner life all we can depend on is the state of our mind. We must remember that we may applaud a person for what he has achieved, but we respect him for who he is. "To be" is more important than "to have." We have divided the world into the "haves" and "have-nots" and continue to honor those who "have." As long as we persist in doing this, society will continue to degrade, because we are not looking at what man "is" but what he "has."

Here is a very poignant story of a rich brother and a poor sister. The affluent man was very arrogant and would not invite his sister to his home. Despite his lack of courtesy, the poor sister decided to visit her brother one day, along with her children. The brother insulted her and told her to leave his house. Saddened by his behavior, she prayed to God for help. As a result of His blessings she gained a great deal of wealth. The brother heard of this change of fortune and invited his sister to his house for a feast. The sister went to his house, beautifully dressed and laden with ornaments. When the food was served, she took off all her ornaments and started feeding them. The brother was outraged and asked her what she was doing. Totally unfazed, she replied that she was feeding those symbols of wealth that were the basis for his invitation. A man may be worth a million dollars, but still be worthless. As long as outer wealth is given more importance than inner wealth, inner values will continue to degrade. We have to understand that there is a difference between "is" and "has." The former is more important.

Three Aspects of Universal Consciousness

Brahman —the Infinite Reality — is indicated by the term *saccidānanda*. *Sat, cit,* and *ānanda* are three aspects of the Universal Consciousness. They are one and the same and form the basis of all values. Therefore, we should not create divisions. *Sat* is existence or "isness." All beings want to live and live forever. Therefore, respect for life is a value. Value lies in saving a life, not merely in refraining from killing. We have the story of Gautama Buddha and his cousin. The cousin shot the bird, but Buddha saved its life. Both the boys claimed the bird as theirs. If the bird were asked, whom she belonged to, would she not opt for her savior?

Cit is knowledge. We do not want to be exploited, but have no qualms about exploiting other people's ignorance. One man was selling watches at a very low price. Someone asked him, how he could make a profit if he sold the watches at such low prices. He replied that he would make money by repairing the watches. He knew that the watches were defective, so he sold them at prices that were impossible to match anywhere else. In similar ways we deceive people.

Ānanda is the happiness that each one of us desires. I want to live happily and so does every one else. So what right do we have to destroy or take away the happiness of another?

The one who works for unity truly works for the propagation of inner values. Divide and rule has been the way of the world. We are very good at dividing ourselves and letting others rule. Material objects and gains are the reason for the division of political parties and families. It is not that we do not know about the inner virtues or values, but we give more importance to outer things.

A very famous verse (*śloka*) from the *Mahābhārata* says that man is a slave to money, but money is slave to none. Knowing all this, we still say superficially that we detest corruption and that honesty is the best policy. But we remain highly distrustful. At government levels we have agencies that monitor the work of other departments. Despite this, corruption still continues, because even the people charged with vigilance are open to corruption. When honesty and trust are absent, corruption will persist. As long as we give greater importance to power, pleasure, and money, inner values will take a back seat. We must stand up for the greater values in life, or else we will fall for everything that comes.

Lastly, we must know why we need to follow the greater values. Some people say that there is no need for religion or God, that just the observance of human values is enough. But human values have real meaning only when they are dedicated to a higher goal. We generally dedicate our activities to our loved ones. Authors dedicate their books to their parents, teachers, and so forth. The act of dedication adds new meaning to the action. Similarly, a value can be sustained only if it is offered at a higher altar.

Take the example of a businessman who follows the values of punctuality, efficient service, and honesty in order to make his business more prosperous. Once his credibility is established, he tends to relax, which causes the business to decline. Why is this? The work has not been dedicated to a higher ideal. People will be able to sustain a virtuous life only when the values and virtues they uphold are dedicated for inner purification, God-Realization, or devotion to God. Then only can one persevere in the midst of obstacles and hindrances. Often people want to know how long they need to be patient or loyal, or how many times they need to be forgiving, but can we really put a limit on these qualities?

Values have real meaning only when they are dedicated to God. The saint, Meera Bai, and other saints were put through innumerable hardships, but they did not budge because their ideals or goals were not material. They did not seek appreciation or reciprocation from anyone. To sustain the values there has to be a high altar of dedication. Such an altar in life will alter our life.

We call ourselves the roof and crown of creation. Therefore, we must prove ourselves worthy of this high calling. The rich must look after the welfare of the poor and make sure they also become prosperous. The superior must protect the inferior and the more powerful must look after the weaker. Such actions alone will add value to our lives. Otherwise we will add years to our lives and not life to our years. Our lives must be vibrant so that they are a blessing to others and to ourselves.

XXII

Practicing Religion Scientifically

by Paramahansa Yogananda

[From a talk given at First Self-Realization Fellowship Temple, Encinitas, California, February 18, 1940]

It is often said that there is a great conflict between science and religion. It is true that scientists look doubtfully at the scriptural statement that "the heaven and the earth" were created in a matter of days. From their practical studies of the earth and the heavens, they have proved that creation came into being through a slow evolutionary process; and that the progression of earth alone, from gases to matter, plants, animal life, and man, required millions of years. So there is a great deal of difference between the findings of the scientists and a literal interpretation of the scriptural texts.

One of the virtues of the true scientist is that he is open-minded. Working from a little data, he experiments until he uncovers verifiable principles of nature and how they work; then he gives to the world the result of his investigations. And he is willing to consider and to research further any new evidence that comes to light. It is the efforts of such scientists that have resulted in the discovery of all the natural laws that have been harnessed for the benefit of the world today. Gradually we are learning to use these laws in an ever-widening range of practical ways; as for example in the numerous conveniences in our homes.

Scientists are often branded as materially minded because their questioning of unproved religious beliefs. But God does not condemn them for that. His universal laws operate with impartial justice regardless of man's beliefs. In this sense God is not a respecter of persons but a respecter of law. He has given us free will, and whether we worship Him or not, if we respect His laws, we shall receive the beneficial results of such regard. A doubting scientist might explain his position in this way: "Even if I don't believe in God, I do try to do what is right. If there is a God, He will reward or punish me according to my respect for His laws. And if there is no God, since I am obeying the laws I find to be true, surely I shall receive any benefit there from."

So, whether or not they are godless, or making their efforts for material gain, those scientists whose researches are uncovering more and more of God's laws are nonetheless working in cooperation with Him to do some good for the world.

Belief Is Only the First Step

Law governs everything in the universe; yet most people have never tried to apply the scientific law of experimentation and research to test religious doctrines. They simply believe, thinking it impossible to investigate and prove the scriptural texts. "We have only to believe," they assure themselves and others; and that is to be accepted as all there is to religion. But the Bible tells us that "Faith is the *substance* of things hoped for, the *evidence* of things not seen."[1] Faith is different from belief, which is only the first step. If I were to tell you that behind this building there is a huge lion, you would probably say, "We don't see how it could be possible!" But if I insisted, "Yes, there is a lion there," you would believe me to the extent that you would go out and investigate. Belief was necessary in order to make you look into it — and if you didn't see the lion, you would say that I had told you a story! Similarly, if I want to persuade you to make a spiritual experiment, you have to believe me before you will carry it out. You can believe, at least, until you prove differently.

Faith, however, cannot be contradicted: it is intuitive conviction of truth, and it cannot be shaken even by contrary evidence. Faith can heal the sick, raise the dead, create new universes. Jesus said, "If ye have faith as a grain of mustard seed, ye shall say unto this mountain, Remove hence to yonder place; and it shall remove; and nothing shall be impossible unto you." [2]

Science is reasonable, willing to alter its views in the light of new facts. It is skeptical about religion only because it has not experimented in that field; although it is now beginning such research at Harvard. Experimental psychology has greatly advanced, and is doing its utmost to understand the inner man. Machines have been invented that can record the different kinds of emotion man experiences; it is said that if one lies while being tested on a polygraph, he usually cannot conceal the fact, no matter how hard he tries.

Putting Religion into Practice

Scientific knowledge is built upon facts. The medical side is fairly well developed, though the causes and cures of certain ailments are yet to be discovered. But what science does know, it is more or less sure about, because the various factors concerned have been tested: theories have been tried and proven. In religion it is different. People are given certain facts or truths and told to believe them. After a little while, when their belief is not fulfilled, doubt creeps in; and then they go from religion to religion trying to find proof. You hear about God in churches and temples; you can read about Him in books; but you can *experience* God only through Self-realization attained by practicing definite scientific techniques. In India, religion is based upon such scientific methods. Realization is what India specialized in, and those who want to know God should learn her methods; they are not India's sole property. Just as electricity was discovered in the West, and we in India benefit from it; so India has discovered the ways by which God can be known, and the West should profit by them. By experimentation, India has proved the truths in religion. In the future, religion everywhere will be a matter of experimentation; it will not be based solely upon belief.

Millions of people are changing from one church to another without truly believing in their hearts what they have heard about God. They say, "Well, I pray, but most of the time He does not respond." Nevertheless, God is always aware of us. He knows all about us, yet we remain absolutely ignorant of Him. This is the cause of the various kinds of doubts that play upon our minds. If God is, we must be able to know Him. Why should we merely read and hear discussions about Him, and yet know nothing from personal experience?

Yet there is a definite way to experience God. And what is that way? It is scientific experimentation with religious truths. And put into practice what you believe! It is possible to put religion into practice, to use it as a science that you can prove by experimenting on yourself. The search for Truth is the most marvelous search in the world. Instead of being merely a matter of attending a Sunday service or performing one's *pūjā,*[3] religion must have a practical side. Learn how to build your life around spiritual ideals. Without practical application, religion is of little value.

A man who used to own a ranch near here was quite materialistic. I urged him to come to Encinitas from time to time, and he did so. After the first few visits, he said, with tears in his eyes, "I never realized there was a place whose very atmosphere could speak so much of God's presence." You see, religion must be practical. It must create some change in you — in your consciousness, and in your behavior. All those who have been coming here regularly have changed their lifestyle for the better. They have been spiritually influenced by this environment.

So religion must be experimented with, to prove it and make it practical. Many churches do great social good, but they do not show you how you can actually prove God to yourself, and how you can be in tune with Him.

Experience Silence

The first experiment with religion must begin with silence. Most people never take time to be silent or to sit quietly in meditation.

Hours and hours I remain in inner silence. When I am with people, I enjoy them immensely; I am with them fully and wholeheartedly. But when I am away from people, I am entirely alone in that supreme joy of life — the bliss of God. No matter where I am, that joy of God is always with me. Why don't you experiment with silence, so that you can live in this same way? Most of you can't sit still for even ten minutes without your thoughts running away in all directions. You have not learned to be at peace in your home within, because you are always restlessly chasing about in your mind. My master, Shri Yukteswar, used to say: "Locking the door of the storehouse of happiness, man runs everywhere else, begging for that happiness. How foolish, when he has the whole store of joy lying within himself!" From my childhood I sought God, and communion with Him has given me happiness that no fulfilled material desires could ever give. You have nothing if you have not God. You have everything if you have God; for He is the Master of the universe.

If you haven't felt any results from religion, experiment in meditation. Shake God out of His silence. You must insist: "Lord, speak to me!" If you make a supreme effort in the silence of the night and in the early morning, after a little while you will see a glimmer of God's light or feel a ripple of His joy coming over your consciousness. Experimenting to know God in meditation, in silence, brings the most real, most remarkable results.

Scientists once thought that water was a single element. But experiments later proved that two invisible elements, hydrogen and oxygen, come together in a certain combination to make up water. Similarly, by religious experiment, wonderful spiritual truths are realized. When you sit quietly in meditation, and your mind is withdrawn within, you will have proof of God and of your own true nature. Experimentation with religious laws is marvelous because the result doesn't take place outside yourself; it is right within you.

Truthfulness

Only the application of religious methods can bring lasting happiness. One of the most important spiritual principles to apply is truthfulness. The meaning of truth is not clearly understood by most people. Truth is in exact correspondence with Reality; hence its end result is always good. Those who develop the habit of telling little lies all the time will find it hard ever to be wholly truthful in any statement. Such chronic liars never think of the importance of speaking truth; they don't even realize they are lying. Their own imagination becomes truth to them, and they can no longer see the real truth in any situation.

Many who do not understand the importance of speaking truth rationalize their deceptions by saying, "Well, if I always tell the truth I am sure to be gypped, because the rest of the world doesn't work that way. A little lie now and then enables me to get along beautifully." How sad!

To be always truthful we must understand the difference between fact and truth. If you see a crippled man and, reasoning that his lameness is an obvious fact, you greet him, "How do you do, Mr. Lame Man!" you will offend him. Your truthfully pointing out his defect only hurt; it did no good. Therefore, one should not speak unpleasant *facts* unnecessarily, even though they be true.

However, if for good reason you don't want to speak the truth, at least don't tell a lie! Suppose you are meditating in a corner, believing you are hidden from sight. Your desire is that nobody know what you are doing. But someone discovers you and calls out, "Hello! What are you doing?" And to hide the fact that you were meditating, you reply, "I was eating a banana." To tell such a lie is unnecessary. You could have replied, "I am busy now, and I don't want to be disturbed." This truthful statement is much better than even a little lie to shield from others' curiosity the fact of what you were doing. It is this type of lying that most people get into. Avoid it, because it encourages a habit pattern of being untruthful, even when there is no need to evade the truth.

It is also wrong to speak the truth when, by doing so, one betrays another person unnecessarily and to no good purpose. Suppose a man drinks, but tries to hide it from the rest of the world. You know about his weakness, and so in the name of truthfulness you announce to your friends, "You know that so and so drinks, don't you?" Such a remark is uncalled for; one should not be busy about other people's business. Be protective about others' personal faults, so long as they harm no one else. Speak privately to an offender about his failings, if you have an opportunity or responsibility to help him; but never, under pretext of helping someone, speak deliberately to hurt him. You will only "help" him to become your enemy. You may also extinguish any desire that he might have had to become better.

Truth is always wholesome; fact can sometimes be harmful. However true it may be, a fact that goes against good is only a fact; it is not truth. Never reveal unpleasant facts that cause meaningless suffering to someone else, such as speaking out unnecessarily against another's character. This is often done to well-known persons by sensation-seeking newspapers or magazines. The motive is to hurt the individual's reputation, or to reap personal gain at his expense. Do not bring upon yourself the bad karma that results from revealing harmful facts against others, when no true or noble purpose is served thereby. When you must evade revealing some unpleasant fact, be sure you also avoid implying what you are trying to hide. After all, God is forgiving; and we, His children, should be forgiving. Why should you be the medium of someone else's harm? Your hurtful action will rebound and harm you, too. We have to live through the results of every experience we put others through. There are men who live in peace, and there are men who live in worry and unhappiness. The latter have not had the wisdom to experiment and discover how it is possible to live in peace. Otherwise, they would have learned not to tell untruths and not to talk against others in a mean and harmful way.

Learning to be Unselfish

Learn also to be unselfish. To find happiness in making others happy is a true goal of one who loves God. Giving happiness to others is tremendously important to our own happiness, and a most satisfying experience. Some people think only of their own family: "Us four and no more." Others think only of self: "How am I going to be happy?" But these are the very persons who do not become happy!

It is not right to seek personal happiness regardless of others' well-being. If you unscrupulously take away others' dollars for yourself, you may become rich, but you will never be happy, because their thoughts of resentment against you will react upon you. The divine law is that whenever you try to make yourself happy at the cost of others' welfare, everyone will want to make you unhappy. But if you try to make others happy, even at the cost of your own contentment, everyone will think of your welfare. Whenever you think of your own necessities, remember the needs of others, too. As soon as you feel concerned for their well-being, you will want to make them happy. The unselfish person gets along beautifully with his family and with the rest of the world. The selfish person always gets into trouble and loses his peace of mind.

Self-Control

Religious experimentation will show you that an uncontrolled existence, also, is the way to misery. The individual who lives all the time in an undisciplined manner is constantly filled with restlessness and worries. But he who has learned self-control knows the way to real happiness.

Whenever you reason that you cannot do without something, you have become its slave. The secret of happiness is to be master of yourself. Many of the things you shouldn't do, you want to do. But when you have cultivated the power to control your desire to do something, even though you are tempted to do it, you have self-mastery. Most people need to develop "won't power"; it enables you to avoid doing things you shouldn't do. When you say, "I won't give in to this wrong habit," and you don't, that is self-mastery. "Won't power" develops strength of mind.

Man's outer behavior reflects his inner life. External luxuries cannot make the soul happy; it is only by control of one's life that the soul experiences happiness and peace. Every morning when I get up, I make certain resolutions, and then throughout the day I mentally whip myself to be sure that I fulfill them. This develops great will power; and when I see all my resolutions carried out, I feel I am a conqueror. So practice self-control. If you don't, you will find yourself constantly carried away on the waves of emotion.

Practice religion every day of your life. On Sundays you learn about the divine law of forgiveness: if you are slapped on the left cheek, turn the right cheek also. But do you practice this in everyday life? or do you think it is foolish to do so? Experiment. When you retaliate by giving the other person a slap, you feel terrible; your action is just as bad as the other person's. Anger and bitterness react not only upon your mind, but upon your physical body. You feel a great heat in your brain, which upsets your nervous system. Why should you take on the contagion of the hatred of him who slaps you? Why should you disrupt your mental peace? Isn't it better to be able to say: "I am happy within myself because, in spite of your blows, I have done no harm to you and have wished you well." Though it is easier to slap in return for a slap, remember that the aftereffects of such a reaction — loss of mental peace, and physiological disturbance — are not worth the momentary satisfaction of revenge. When you refrain from retaliating, you will find that you have calmed down your enemy also; whereas if you hit back, you only rouse his emotions more.

So to be in control of your emotions is important to happiness. Then no one can get you angry, no one can make you jealous. You stand unchallenged in your own consciousness. You know what you are. You have experimented with your thoughts, and you know what treasure of peace you have within.

Worry doesn't help you, either. Not only does it burn out your nerves, leaving you cranky and cross all the time; it puts an extra strain on the heart. When you leave your work for the day, forget it; do not pick it up mentally and carry it home with you. Worry only clouds your mind so that you cannot think clearly. You should learn to rely more on God. This is a science, a divine law. There is always a way out of your trouble; and if you take the time to think clearly, to think how to get rid of the cause of your anxiety instead of just worrying about it, you become a master.

Many people come to me to talk about their worries. I urge them to sit quietly, meditate, and pray; and after feeling calmness within, to think of the alternate ways by which the problem can be solved or eliminated. When the mind is calm in God, when the faith is strong in God, they find a solution to their problem. Merely ignoring problems won't solve them, but neither will worrying about them. Meditate until you become calm; then put your mind on your problem and pray deeply for God's help. Concentrate on the problem and you will find a solution without going through the terrible strain of worry.

The Working of God's Laws

A prayer that is strong and deep will definitely receive God's answer. But if you do not make any real effort to pray to Him, naturally you will not feel any response. At one time or another, everyone has found some desire fulfilled through prayer. When your will is very strong it touches the Father, and the Father wills that your desire be fulfilled. When *He* wills, all nature takes notice. God does respond when you deeply pray to Him with faith and determination. Sometimes He answers by dropping a thought in the mind of another person who can fulfill your desire or need; that individual then serves as God's instrument to bring about the desired result.

You don't realize how wonderfully this great power works. It operates mathematically. There is no "if" about it. And that is what the Bible means by faith: it is *proof* of things unseen.

If you practice the presence of God, you will know that what I am saying is truth. Go to God; pray and cry to Him until He shows the workings of His laws to you and guides you. Remember, greater than a million reasonings of the mind is to sit and meditate upon God until you feel calmness within. Then say to the Lord, "I can't solve my problem alone, even if I thought a zillion different thoughts; but I can solve it by placing it in Your hands, asking first for Your guidance, and then following through by thinking out the various angles for a possible solution." God does help those who help themselves.

When your mind is calm and filled with faith after praying to God in meditation, you are able to see various answers to your problems; and because your mind is calm, you are capable of picking out the best solution. Follow that solution, and you will meet with success. This is applying the science of religion in your daily life.

Seeing is Believing

Everything that is visible is the result of the Invisible. Because you do not see God, you do not believe He is here. Yet every tree and every blade of grass is controlled by the power of God within it. That Power is not visible externally. What you see are merely the results coming from the Power in the seeds planted in the earth, which emerge as the tree and the blades of grass. You do not see what is going on within, in the factory of the Infinite. Every object in this universe, and every potential therein, has been produced first in the factory of the mind of God; and God sublets that power to the factory of the mind of man. From that little factory of man's mind comes everything he accomplishes — great books, intricate machines, outstanding achievements in any walk of life. Above all, in that mind-factory lies man's unique ability to find God.

The mind is a perfect instrument of knowledge when you have learned to base your life on truth. Then you see everything in a clear, undistorted way, exactly as it is. Therefore, learn to experiment with this mind. Learn to follow the science of religion and you can become the greatest kind of scientist, the greatest kind of inventor, the master of your own fate.

If you can just remember and apply the truths I have told you, there is nothing you cannot accomplish in life. And the greatest of all achievements is to find God. By the application of science in religion, your uncertain belief in spiritual possibilities can become realization of their highest fulfillment. Then you will be the most successful of all human beings, greater than all the scientists on earth. The great ones who have discovered

Him never live in doubt; they experience the truth. "Ye shall know the truth, and the truth shall make you free." [4] You have everything when you have found God.

FOOTNOTES:

[1]   Hebrews 11:1.
[2]   Matthew 17:20.
[3]   Ritual worship performed by Hindus.
[4]   John 8:32.

XXIII

Vedanta:
A Universal Message
by Swami Prabhavananda

Vedanta does not conflict with the ideals of the Western man.
It is in accord with the Western spirit of science and rationalism and also the ideal of humanistic ethics.

The Renaissance brought to the West simultaneous growth in
political freedom, economic prosperity, intellectual advancement, and social reform. Earthly life became once more the
object of existence, and religion was made subservient to it.

The Greek spirit of science and rationalism became predominant during this period and eventually led to the great development in scientific investigation and research, which has
characterized the life of the western man from the Renaissance
to the present age.

Today, an increasing number of earnest and thoughtful people feel that science by itself cannot solve their basic problems;
and that the knowledge it can give does not bring lasting peace.
They believe that religion alone can end the present crisis in the
life of modern man. But what kind of religion?

We have seen fanaticism, persecution, and war result when
free inquiry is banned and reason stifled to uphold a religion
that teaches acceptance of authority on blind faith. Moreover,
there are so many contending sects, each claiming that it alone
has the key to the truth of God. Which are we to choose?

Vedanta is not a particular religion but a philosophy, which includes the basic truths of all religions. It teaches that man's real nature is divine; that it is the aim of man's life on earth to unfold and manifest the hidden Godhead within him; and that Truth is universal. The truth of God exists eternally. Each one of us has to discover this truth within his own heart. Is our hunger appeased if someone else eats for us?

It is not by accepting a prophet or by believing in a dogma that we are saved but by experiencing the truth of God for ourselves.

Vedanta is not antagonistic to the Western spirit of science and rationalism, because the revelation of truth does not contradict another truth. Although reason cannot reach that knowledge, this does not mean that reason and intellect are to be stifled. On the contrary, reason and intellect are elevated and expanded through the practice of spiritual disciplines, and then the truth of God becomes revealed.

The Western ideal of humanistic ethics is also not to be ignored. The welfare of the body and mind must be taken into account. But consider what man really is and what his *dharma* is. Man is not a conglomeration of body, senses, and the mind that communicates with an extra-cosmic being, which is God. He is fundamentally spirit and has a body and mind.

Thus Vedanta emphasizes and directs our minds towards the same truth that was also taught by Moses and Christ — that "the kingdom of God is within." And we have to enter that kingdom and unfold our latent divinity. We are one in spirit.

Meditation Essential

A widespread misunderstanding exists in the West with regard to Vedanta in its emphasis upon meditation. People often say that it is all right for Orientals to close their eyes and try to find God within, but that Western minds are different and that it is not possible for them to meditate. Many sincere and earnest people are of this opinion.

But Vedanta and Christianity both emphasize the truth that meditation is essential. Saint Paul taught his followers to "pray without ceasing." Where is the truth of our being? Within ourselves. And how can we find that which is within by looking outside? Thus meditation is fundamental in spiritual life. It is wrong to say that the western mind cannot meditate. The West could not have made its progress in science or any other field of life without meditation which is an unbroken flow of thought towards the object of concentration.

No sense pleasure, no economic or cultural success is possible without concentrated thought. But there is a difference. In the West the end is outward achievement and meditation the means. As a result of making external accomplishments the goal, we have atom bombs today and live in constant fear.

True, we must satisfy our bodily desires and we must develop our mental powers, but for what purpose? To realize God. He must be made the end, not the means. Christ taught — "Lay not for yourselves treasures upon earth, where moth and rust doth corrupt, and where thieves break through and steal, but lay up for yourselves treasures in heaven, where neither moth nor rust doth corrupt, and where thieves do not break through nor steal."

Our attitude must change. We must be active, we must work, but let us work for God and dedicate our actions to Him. Eventually, through meditation and selfless actions the law of our being becomes revealed to us, and we become fearless. That is the state of attainment each one of us can reach.

Personal Experience

The question may arise — what about the creeds, dogmas, and rituals of the various religions? Should they be discarded? Vedanta says that this is not necessary. Have as many creeds, dogmas, and rituals as you like, but consider whether they are helping you to realize God. If not, throw them overboard. Doctrines, books, and symbols are only secondary details. The main thing is to realize God. Whatever helps you to unfold the divinity within you is right; whatever prevents you from realizing your true nature is wrong.

Each individual has a particular path to follow, depending on his stage of development, but the goal, the divine unfoldment, is the same for all. This is true for nations as well as individuals. From ancient times it has been taught in the *Vedas,* "Truth is one, but its expressions are many." If we can understand this principle and apply it in our everyday life, we will have cooperation instead of competition.

This truth of Vedanta does not conflict with the ideals of Western man. Only the Western tendency to insist on one path for all, whether in the field of material or spiritual culture, must be given up. If we assimilate the Vedantic concept of unity in variety, we can learn to live together harmoniously with different cultures, different ideologies, and different religions. Let there be variety in every department of life. At the same time let us recognize the underlying oneness in spirit. That is the only way to find peace.

Thus Vedanta preaches a universal message, the message of harmony. In its insistence on personal experience of the truth of God, on the divinity of man, and the universality of Truth, it has kept the spirit of religion alive since the age of the Vedas.

The ideal religion "will be a religion which will have no place for persecution or intolerance in its polity which will recognize divinity in every man and woman, and whose whole scope, whose whole force, will be centered in aiding humanity to realize its own true, divine nature."

Every religion is a path to reach the same goal. One who has attained this goal is no longer a follower of a particular path or a particular religion. He has become a man of God and a blessing to mankind.

XXIV

Science and Vedanta

by Swami Mukhyananda

> The difference between Vedanta and Science is this: Science
> tries to prove, I who create Science am a zero; hence, Science,
> the creation of a zero is a zero. Vedanta upholds, I am in my
> real nature, Divine, the All. I am the One to which zeros,
> represented by Science, are added and get their meaning and
> increasing value.

Einstein has stated: "Religion without Science is blind and Science without Religion is lame." That is the view of a liberal
scientist, who recognizes the necessity of both, though with his
own concepts of Religion and Science. We would, however,
reverse it and put it according to our ancient formulation by the
Samkhya philosophers, which seems to be more appropriate:

> *Prakṛti* (*insentient* Matter/Nature), and the Material Science
> built exclusively upon it, *is blind* (spiritually); and *Puruṣa* (the
> *conscious* Spirit), and the Spiritual Science built only upon it,
> *is lame* (materially); but by a combination of both (specially
> in empirical matters), the Spirit (*Puruṣa*) will guide Matter,
> and Matter (*Prakṛti*) will accomplish things — like the lame
> person sitting on the shoulder of the blind person and guid-
> ing him, and the blind person doing the walking.

This is called in Sanskrit *Andha-Paṅgu Nyāya* (the Maxim of
the Blind and the Lame), by the *Samkhya* philosophers.

We find absolutely no contradiction between Vedanta and
Science, though their fields of investigation and viewpoints

may differ. They are complementary, not contradictory. Swami Vivekananda was the greatest advocate of the combination of Vedanta and Science. The imaginary contradiction is seen only due to misunderstanding or lack of proper study of Vedanta and Science in their true spirit and perspective as investigative sciences in the realm of Spirit and Matter. Thus Material Science, leading to *Abhyudaya*, or worldly welfare, must be founded on the Spiritual Science (Vedanta), which leads to *Niḥśreyasa* (Spiritual *Summum Bonum*).[1]

In conclusion, we may say that Modern Western Science investigates only a part of the universe, the physical universe, external to man, excluding the investigation into human personality, the real investigator. It takes the empirical view of man and tries to increase his knowledge of the external sensible world and make his physical life comfortable by the control and manipulation of environment, materials, forces, and energies through technology. It does not go into the fundamental questions of the origin, nature, and meaning of the universe in itself and its purpose; or of the nature of man, life and its purpose, and the final Goal of man; or of ethics, morality, aesthetics, peace, and other values; nor does it concern itself with the realization of the Ultimate Spiritual Reality within the core of human personality and self-fulfillment. In short, it functions within the limits of empirical framework and investigates the external universe as an object of the empirical man. It gives us, so to say, a skeletal universe.

Being *ad hoc* in its approach, Modern Western Science does not look into the long-range consequences and effects of its technological applications on human mind, social life, and ecology, and, as a result, while it solves one problem, it creates several others more pervasive in their harmful effects, as is often seen.

On the other hand, while maintaining a scientific and rational approach, Vedanta is a full scientific philosophy of Reality, life, and existence, and is a great support of morality, ethics, aesthetics, and religion. It gives physical science its due place in life. It reveals that the true nature of man is Divine and helps him to realize it and manifest it in life through Yogic Paths. It is deeply concerned with the Secular and spiritual human values (the Four *Puruśārtha*: *Dharma* — Ethics and Religion; *Artha* — Prosperity and culture; *Kāma* — Fulfillment of legitimate Desires and Aesthetics; and *Mokṣa* — Spiritual Freedom and Enlightenment through Realization of the Ultimate Reality, one's divine Self). It shows the solidarity of all life and existence and integrates the secular and the spiritual in a harmonious manner leading man ultimately to Spiritual Liberation (*Mokṣa* or *Mukti*) from the bonds of matter, and to the Supreme Goal — the identity of one's real nature with the Infinite Divine.

A harmonious combination of Vedanta and Science will raise humanity to a higher level of culture and fuller ideal in life and lead man to fulfillment both in secular and spiritual fields by helping him to attain *Ahhyudaya* (Secular Advancement) and *Niḥśreyasa* (Spiritual Fulfillment), the *Summurn Bonum*, based on *Dharma* (Ethics and Morality).

FOOTNOTE:

[1] Some "scientists," forgetting that the Modern Western Science is "Science" only in a restricted sense, and that it is not a comprehensive science of total reality, think that their Science is the sole standard of entire knowledge, and consider all mental and spiritual sciences to be mere superstitions. This is against the true scientific spirit. One should not make an "ISM" such as "SCIENTISM" of Science. True Science should be an open system, and comprehensive, like the Vedanta, and not a closed circle.

About the Authors

Benson, Herbert

Herbert Benson, M.D., is the founding President of the Mind/ Body Medical Institute and the Mind/Body Medical Institute Associate Professor of Medicine, Harvard Medical School. A graduate of Wesleyan University and the Harvard Medical School, Dr. Benson is the author or co-author of more than 170 scientific publications and ten books.

Capra, Fritjof

Fritjof Capra, Ph.D., physicist and systems theorist, is a founding director of the Center for Eco-literacy, California, which promotes ecology and systems thinking in primary and secondary education. Dr. Capra is on the faculty of Schumacher College, an international center for ecological studies in England, and frequently gives management seminars for top executives. He is the author of several international bestsellers, including *The Tao of Physics, The Turning Point,* and *The Web of Life.* His most recent book, *The Hidden Connections,* was published this year.

Chaudhuri, Haridas

Haridas Chaudhuri possibly the greatest exponent of integral yoga since Sri Aurobindo, Haridas Chaudhuri authored the Quest books, *Mastering the Problems of Living, Being, Evolution and Immortality*, and *Integral Yoga.* Until his passing he was the President of the California Institute of Asian Studies in San Francisco.

The Dalai Lama

H.H. The Dalai Lama is the spiritual and temporal leader of the Tibetan people. His tireless efforts on behalf of human rights and world peace have brought him international recognition. He is a recipient of the Wallenberg Award (conferred by the U. S. Congressional Human Rights Foundation), the Albert Schweitzer Award and the Nobel Peace Prize.

Dossey, Larry

Larry Dossey, M.D., is a physician of internal medicine. He was a battalion surgeon in Vietnam, chief of staff at medical City Dallas Hospital, and a member of Hillary Rodham Clinton's Task Force on Health Care Reform. He has lectured all over the world, including at the Mayo Clinic, Harvard, Johns Hopkins, Cornell, and numerous other major universities and medical schools. His eight other books include *Space, Time & Medicine*; *Healing Words;* and *Prayer Is Good Medicine.*

Dunlap, Rebekah Alezander

Rebekah Alezander Dunlap is a retired Unity minister and author. She was ordained as a Unity Minister in 1976 and served Unity churches in the U.S. until her retirement in 1998. During her tenure as a minister, Rebekah pioneered three Unity ministeries.

Frawley David

Dr. David Frawley (Pandit Vamadeva Shastri) is the author of an entire series of books on Ayurvedic medicine including *Yoga and Ayurveda, Ayurveda and the Mind* and the *Yoga of Herbs.* He has also written extensively on Yoga, Vedic Astrology and related Vedic disciplines. Dr. Frawley is one of the few westerners whose expertise on these subjects is honored throughout India. He is currently director of the American Institute of Vedic Studies, which offers courses and training programs in Ayurveda and related Vedic disciplines and president of the American Council of Vedic Astrology.

Goswami, Amit

Amit Goswami, Ph.D., was born in India and earned his doctorate in theoretical nuclear physics from Calcutta University in 1964; He has been a professor of physics at the University of Oregon since 1968. A senior scholar in residence at the Institute of Noetic Sciences, Goswami regularly teaches at the Holmes Institute in Los Angeles; UNIPAZ in Brazil; the Theosophical Society in America at Wheaton, Illinois; the Holma College of Holistic Studies in Sweden; and the Sivananda International Yoga and Vedanta Centers. Amit Goswami lives with his wife Uma Krishnamurthy in San Rafael, California and Bangalore, India.

Harpur, Tom

Tom Harpur, columnist for *The Toronto Star*, Rhodes scholar and Anglican priest, is a prominent writer on religious and ethical issues. He is the author of seven best-selling books including *For Christ's Sake*, and *Would You Believe?* He has hosted numerous radio and television programs, including *Life After Death,* a ten-part series based on his best-selling book of the same name, and a six-part television series based on his bestseller *The Uncommon Touch: An Investigation of Spiritual Healing.*

McFarlane, Thomas J.

Thomas J. McFarlane was raised in rural Oregon. He studied liberal arts at the University of Oregon Honors College, physics at Stanford University and mathematics at the University of Washington. He is now in the graduate program in Philosophy and Religion at the California Institute of Integral Studies, and is a senior partner at a patent firm in Palo Alto, California.

Radhakrishnan, S.

Dr. S. Radhakrishnan (1888-1975), philosopher, humanist, educationist, and religious thinker, was one of those few great men of this century who distinguished themselves equally in the fields of knowledge as well as that of statesmanship. He was the Vice-President (1952-61) and the President of India from 1961-1967. He has a large number of books on religion and philosophy to his credit.

Smith, Huston

Huston Smith, Professor Emeritus of Philosophy, Syracuse University, is considered the country's preeminent public scholar of world religions. He has been profiled in a PBS series by Bill Moyers and appears frequently on National TV and radio.

Swami Chinmayananda

Swami Chinmayananda, the founder of Chinmaya Mission, was a sage and visionary. He toured tirelessly all around the world giving discourses and writing commentaries on the scriptural knowledge of Vedanta, until he left his bodily form in 1993. (See write-up at the end of this book.)

Swami Jitatmananda

Swami Jitatmananda (born 1941) is a monk of the Ramakrishna order. He worked in the mission's various centers as headmaster, and principal, Deputy Director of the School of Foreign Languages in the Hyderabad center, and as the editor of the *Prabuddha Bharata*, the monthly English journal started by Swami Vivekananda in 1896.

ABOUT THE AUTHORS

Swami Mukhyananda

Swami Mukhyananda, joined the Ramakrishna Order formally at its Karachi Center in 1943. He served in different capacities in several centers of the Ramakrishna Math and Mission, including in the editorial department of the Order's journal *Prabhuddha Bharata*, besides acting as the Assistant Minister for two years at the Ramakrishna Vedanta Center in London. During his long association with the Ramakrishna Order of over 60 years, he had the opportunity to make a comparative study of Vedanta and Science in their higher aspects and their approach to the discovery of the ultimate Reality of Existence.

Swami Prabhavananda

Swami Prabhavananda came to the United States in 1923. He eventually founded the Vedanta Society of Southern California, which grew under his direction to a large collection of dedicated temples and monasteries from Santa Barbara to San Diego. With Christopher Isherwood, Frederick Manchester, and other authors the Swami has published many books on Vedanta, including original translations of the *Bhagavad Gītā*, Upanishads, and Patanjali's *Yoga Sūtra*.

Swami Ranganathananda

Swami Ranganathananda was the president of the Ramakrishna Math and Mission. He was born in 1908 and joined the order at the early age of seventeen. Swami Ranganathananda had been secretary of the Ramakrishna Mission institute of Culture, Director of its School of Humanistic and Cultural Studies, and editor of its monthly journal. In 1986 he became the first recipient of the Indira Gandhi award for National Integration. He had traveled throughout the world enthralling people with his magnificent exposition of India's ageless culture backed by an erudition, which, though firmly rooted in the Indian scriptures, gave due place to the role of science and technology. Swamiji left his bodily form on April 25, 2005.

Swami Tejomayananda

Swami Tejomayananda, the spiritual head of Chinmaya Mission centers worldwide since 1993, is fulfilling the vision of his guru, Swami Chinmayananda. As Mission head, Swami Tejomayananda has already conducted more than 500 *jñāna yajña* worldwide. He has served as dean or *ācārya* of the Sandeepany Institutes of Vedanta, both in India and in California. Fluent in Hindi, Marathi and English, and lecturing and writing commentaries in all three languages he makes even the most complicated Vedantic topics clear to his audience.

Stark, Marg

Marg Stark graduated from Mount Holyoke College, got her masters in journalism from Northwestern University, and a lot of life lessons as the daughter of a liberal Presbyterian minister and the wife of a conservative U.S. naval officer. In 2003, *Metropolitan* magazine selected her as one of San Diego's "40 under 40" most accomplished leaders.

Templeton, John

Sir John Templeton, legendary Wall Street financier and founder of the Templeton Mutual Funds, now devotes his time and energy to funding scientific research in religion spirituality and health, character development, and freedom through the John Templeton Foundation. Knighted in 1987 by Queen Elizabeth II for his philanthropic work, he also funds the Templeton prize, given yearly to an outstanding individual whose research has advanced our understanding of God. He is the author and editor of many books on science and world religions, including *Wisdom from World Religions* and *Possibilities for Over One Hundredfold More Spiritual Information.*

ABOUT THE AUTHORS

Wilber, Ken

Ken Wilber's first book *The Spectrum of Consciousness*, written when he was only twenty-three was hailed as "the most sensible, comprehensive book about consciousness since William James." He is the author of more than a dozen books, including *Grace and Grit; Sex, Ecology, Spirituality*; *A Brief History of Everything* and *The Eye of Spirit*; and his large readership has kept all of his books in print. He lives in Boulder, Colorado.

Raje, Sudhakar

Sudhakar Raje is a journalist and writer living in Mumbai, India. He was former editor of *Organizer* a well-known weekly journal of New Delhi. He has written many articles for various journals and newspapers as well as authored books.

Yogananda, Paramahansa

Paramahansa Yogananda came to the U. S. in 1920 as India's delegate to an International Congress of Religious Liberals. In 1925 he established the Self-Realization Fellowship International headquarters in Los Angeles. Today the spiritual and humanitarian work begun by Paramahansa Yogananda continues under the guidance of one of his foremost disciples, Sri Daya Mata, president of Self-Realization Fellowship. The life and teachings of Sri Yogananda are described in his *Autobiography of a Yogi*.

Pronunciation of Sanskrit Letters

a	(but)	k	(skate)	t	⎰think or	ś	(shove)
ā	(father)	kh	(Kate)	th	⎱third	ṣ	(bushel)
i	(it)	g	(gate)	d	⎰this or	s	(so)
ī	(beet)	gh	(gawk)	dh	⎱there	h	(hum)
u	(suture)	ṅ	(sing)	n	(numb)	ṃ	(nasaliza-
ū	(pool)	c	(chunk)	p	(spin)		tion of
ṛ	(rig)	ch	(match)	ph	(loophole)		preceding
ṝ	(rrrig)	j	(John)	b	(bun)		vowel)
ḷ	no English equiva-lent	jh	(jam)	bh	(rub)	ḥ	(aspira-tion of
		ñ	(bunch)	m	(much)		preceding
		ṭ	(tell)	y	(young)		vowel)
		ṭh	(time)	r	(drama)		
e	(play)	ḍ	(duck)	l	(luck)		
ai	(high)	ḍh	(dumb)	v	(wile/vile)		
o	(toe)	n	(under)				
au	(cow)						

Other Chinmaya Publication Series:

THE *Self-Discovery* SERIES

Meditation and Life
by Swami Chinmayananda

Self-Unfoldment
by Swami Chinmayananda

THE *Hindu Culture* SERIES

The Sanskrit word *Mananam* means reflection. The *Mananam Series* of books is dedicated to promoting the ageless wisdom of Vedanta, with an emphasis on the unity of all religions. Spiritual teachers from different traditions give us fresh, insightful answers to age-old questions so that we may apply them in a practical way to the dilemmas we all face in life. It is published by Chinmaya Mission West, which was founded by Swami Chinmayananda in 1975. Swami Chinmayananda pursued the spiritual path in the Himalayas, under the guidance of Swami Sivananda and Swami Tapovanam. He is credited with the awakening of India and the rest of the world to the ageless wisdom of Vedanta. He taught the logic of spirituality and emphasized that selfless work, study, and meditation are the cornerstones of spiritual practice. His legacy remains in the form of books, audio and video tapes, schools, social service projects, and Vedanta teachers who now serve their local communities all around the world.